Murder in a Different Light

Patricia Driscoll

Murder in a Different Light

Formatting by RikHall.com
Cover design: Dave Fymbo- Limelight Book Covers

Acknowledgements

Nick Klimenko, husband, reader, consultant. L.U.M.T.A.
Heartfelt thanks to my beta readers, Thomas Driscoll, Jo Schultz and Malena Elumaily, for their generous advice and encouragement.

Thanks to Rosie and Harry Walwyn for the use of their family name.

For
Daniel B. Driscoll

Chapter One

Almost three years after her husband Jack died, and a year since she quit her job as a probation officer and purchased Pearl's, a run-down antique lamp shop, in a cozy Cape Cod village, Grace Tolliver sailed into her shop with her latest lamp bargain from the local consignment store stashed under her arm. It was a glorious day, the sun still cool, yet shimmering, with a promise of heat. She shuddered when she spotted her employee Michael Shipworth teetering on the top step of a ladder, vigorously pounding a nail into the wall.

"Hi, Grace," Michael greeted her. "I just finished installing this shelf. The black color is very nice and will be wonderful with those white empire lampshades." The ladder wobbled as Michael turned back to the wall and grasped the shelf for support.

Grace held her breath until Michael steadied himself. She wanted to tell him to get down immediately but they'd had this discussion before, with Michael promising never to use the ladder again. He was the prime salesperson in her shop, Pearl's Antique Lamps and Shades. Problem was, he was not young. Nor middle aged. In fact, he was well past retirement age. At first, Grace figured him to be about seventy years old, however, after checking his employment papers, she found that he was eighty. Her other employee, Bella Benson, was even older than Michael, and had worked at Pearl's for more than thirty years after having seen some hard duty as a nurse during the Korean War. They were the best possible employees in so many ways, but, Grace constantly worried about them, fearing falls, exhaustion or worse. But Michael, diminutive in stature, dragged his stepladder all over the shop, never appearing to fear the heights that he would climb to fetch a shade or a lamp from a high shelf.

"That looks great," Grace said, feeling relief as Michael maneuvered his way down the ladder and planted his tasseled leather shoes on the floor. "Take a look at this alabaster vase I picked up on my way to work. It's going to make a stunning lamp when Bella rewires it." Grace sniffed the air. "Phew. Is something burning? Is someone smoking in here?"

"Bella's smoking a cigar on the back porch."

"I didn't realize Bella smoked anything, let alone cigars."

"It's a sometime thing," Michael said. "She's got company."

"I hope her company is leaving soon because we're supposed to pick up her friends and go hiking in fifteen minutes."

"Bella's hiking group? The Merry Widows? You're way too young for that group. Those women are forty years older than you. I hope you know how to perform CPR," Michael chuckled.

"You might want to join us sometime," Grace suggested, at which Michael rolled his eyes, picked up his ladder and headed for the storage closet without comment.

Grace surveyed the space that now housed Pearl's. When she decided to swap spaces with Beaus' Books and move her shop to the downstairs of the nineteenth century building, she hadn't even begun to appreciate the difficulties presented by its general disorder. Lumber, paint cans, tools and electrical cords were strewn around the floors. The windows were covered with plastic, and sawdust filled the air. Boxes of lamps, tools, and shades were scattered around the shop, many draped in old sheets to keep the dust off. It didn't seem possible that order would ever be found amidst this chaos.

The front door of Pearl's opened, and her youngest employee, Duane Kerbey stumbled in, juggling three large boxes that Grace, when packing up the shop for the move, carefully and optimistically labeled 'Fragile.' Half of a jelly donut protruded from his mouth, and sweat poured from underneath the bandanna that was wrapped around his head. His lank, fair hair was wet and pulled into a stringy ponytail. "Where do you want these, Ms. Tolliver?"

"Just stack them on top of those others." Grace pointed vaguely around the cluttered room, letting the "Ms. Tolliver" salutation go. After all, she'd been trying to convince Duane, her young employee, to call her Grace for the past several months with no success. Sometimes Duane got stuck on something and there was no changing it. Grace was glad she hadn't said anything. She was trying to be less controlling. Trying not to fix what couldn't be fixed. Trying not to be like a former probation officer.

"Don't sweat on the boxes," Michael told Duane. "I'm clearing a space in the chandelier room. You can put them in there for now."

"It's hot and these things are heavy," Duane grumbled as he juggled the boxes affixed with labels marked 'Bella's Stuff.'

She realized they were all tired, and everyone was getting on each other's nerves. There was always some bickering, mostly of the friendly variety among her employees, but with the stress of the move it seemed to be escalating into more testy territory.

The screen door leading to the back porch closed with a thump as Bella, attired in her customary housedress and slippers, strode purposefully across the room in her characteristic bold manner. A large woman, in Grace's opinion a look-alike for Julia Child, Bella was a few inches taller than the man who followed her. He was wearing a multi colored Hawaiian shirt with a pair of red sunglasses dangling from his shirt pocket. His face was tanned and weathered. His thick salt and pepper hair was disheveled, as if he'd been out on a boat or clamming in the bay and his smoky ocean blue eyes fixed intensely on Grace. He was a man who had probably seen better days, but who was still very good looking.

"Grace, this is Ben Walwyn, Imogene's son," Bella said. "He's brought me some photos and knick-knacks that she wanted me to have."

Grace instantly recalled Bella's distress, not long ago, when her closest friend, Imogene, who had served as a nurse with her in Korea, had died after a short illness.

"I'm so sorry to hear that your mother recently passed away," Grace said, extending her hand.

"Thank you," Ben replied, as he appeared to be struggling to focus his eyes on Grace. When he swayed toward her, she detected the odor of alcohol on his breath.

Ben scarcely acknowledged Michael and Duane when Grace introduced them, muttering, after kissing Bella's cheek, that he had to go. As he sauntered down the stairs, a blue truck, brakes screeching, came to a halt in front of the shop, and a man Grace recognized as Mason Crawford leaped out.

Mason was a familiar person around the courthouse, her former place of employment, because he was usually in jail, about to go to jail, or in a courtroom, trying to get out of jail. Now, his face was crimson, and his words were sizzling as he shouted obscenities at Ben.

Mason grabbed Ben around the throat with one hand and put his face close to Ben's. "You double crossed me for the last time, Pal!"

Ben pulled the hand from his neck. "Get over it!" He pushed Mason, causing him to stumble backwards, but Mason was not one to back down so easily. He steadied himself and took a swing at Ben, which Ben easily deflected.

"What do you think you're doing?" Ben demanded. "The courthouse is a block away. I'm not going to jail because of you, so get lost."

Scowling, Mason climbed in his truck. "I'm not done with you yet!" he said, before driving off at a high rate of speed.

Ben gave a one-fingered salute in Mason's direction, put his sunglasses on, slid into his pickup and started the ignition. He stared at Bella and the shop for a minute or two before slowly pulling away from the curb.

"He looks like he's had one too many," Grace said. "I hope he doesn't kill someone on his way home."

Chapter Two

"Salty Cove must be right around here," Grace said as she slowed her car, now occupied by Mary, Sharon, and Phyllis, all members of the Merry Widows hiking group. "Didn't you say it would be on the left?"

"Yes, we're really close," Bella said, peering intently through the windshield.

"When was the last time you were here?"

"A couple of months ago," Bella replied. "I came as often as I could when Imogene was sick. I feel a bit apprehensive, coming here now. Her death, although expected, was difficult for me. I remember her, sitting on the front porch, waiting for me, with cups of jasmine tea and a plate of lemon cookies, served on her pretty white wicker table. We would spend hours talking about our families and our experiences long ago in Korea. She was a delightful person, not without her foibles of course, but so much fun to spend time with." Bella sighed. "Ben said he'll be waiting for us and give us a tour. It's a most remarkable house."

"I hear that Salty Cove is nearly in its original condition," Phyllis said from the back seat. "So many of these historic Cape houses have deteriorated due to age and neglect, slipped into the sea, or remodeled beyond recognition."

It had only been a couple of hours since Grace met an intoxicated Ben Walwyn. When Bella informed her that he had invited the Merry Widows to hike at his place, instead of their planned excursion to Sandy Neck Beach, she was apprehensive. But, Bella and the others were so happy with their new plan that she agreed to drive them the extra distance, so that they could tour the property and have their picnic by the private beach in front of the house. The clear September afternoon promised a beautiful sunset. No reason to feel apprehensive just because Ben's presence at the lamp shop made her uncomfortable. Better to shake off her queasy feelings and enjoy the evening.

"Look, there's a bunch of people standing in the cranberry bog," Mary said. "And there's a small bus. Is that the latest tourist thing? A trip into the bogs?"

"I think so," Grace replied, fondly remembering her trips to Napa and Sonoma during the years she had lived on the west coast. "I guess it's the same idea as walking into the vineyards, people love getting a close look at things they don't necessarily see in their own neighborhoods."

"God Almighty!" Mary screamed as Grace pulled the steering wheel sharply to her right, and the car skidded along the edge of the road skirting a ditch that was deep enough to cause tumult inside the car as its occupants were bounced around in ways that eighty years olds should not have to experience.

"Steady, Grace. You're doing great," Bella said as she bumped alongside Grace.

"What the hell was that?" Grace said as she managed to pull the car to a firm stop inches from a sizable boulder. "Is anyone hurt?"

A few moments of silence caused Grace's heart to race.

"No, we're all okay," Mary said.

Grace let out a huge sigh of relief. "Did anyone see anything? All I saw was a dark car crossing the centerline and barreling down on us."

"I think it was a black van. They are always going too fast," Mary said, as if the same reckless person drove all black vans. "I think I saw something sparkly."

"I didn't see anything," Sharon added. "I was putting my cell phone in my bag, when all of a sudden we were swerving all over the place."

"Whoever it was, they were in a big hurry," Bella said.

"Yes, and they couldn't be bothered to stop to see if we're

all right," Grace said, her voice trembling. After a moment and a few deep breaths, she started up her engine, her fingers shaking on the wheel. "That was a really close call."

Chapter Three

Grace drove slowly up the driveway, a mix of dirt, sand, and gravel, surrounded by thick scrub pines. After a series of lazy turns, the property known as Salty Cove came into view. The house was immense, weathered to a bleak gray, two stories tall, with several dormers and a long, low porch that sagged in the middle above a short flight of stairs.

"Oh my goodness!" the three women in the back seat said in unison.

"Isn't she an old beauty?" Bella said. "Just like us."

"Right you are," piped up Phyllis. "And look at that ocean view!"

As for Grace, she felt herself calming down. The near accident on the road had been frightening, and they were all lucky not to have flipped into the cranberry bog. But, this old house, with its expansive lawns, overgrown as they were, and a view to die for, was having a soothing impact on her nerves. Opening the door to the backseat, she watched as her companions straggled out.

"Ben's around here someplace," Bella said reaching back into the car for her walking stick. "I see his truck over by the garden shed. Why don't we take a walk around? We're bound to find him."

Grace craned her neck to stare up at the house. The roof was uneven, one of many chimneys leaned precariously, and the paint on the trim was peeling. Of course, Grace knew that living by the ocean caused paint to chip and wear off at an alarming speed. Salty Cove had clearly been weathering without intervention for a considerable time.

Bella led the way to a garden gate smothered in ivy, and they stepped into a once lovely kitchen garden, now full of dead herbs and live weeds.

"It used to be so well manicured," she said sadly. "Imogene decided to let the gardeners go because Ben said he could take care of things and save money. Besides, she hoped it would give him something constructive to do. Unfortunately, Ben's idea of taking care of things was quite different from Imogene's. It's still impressive, even if it's not as grand as it was in its heyday."

"It's an absolute dream property. How many acres are we talking about?" Grace asked as she pulled her long chestnut hair off her neck and secured it with a tortoiseshell clip.

"I'm not sure exactly, maybe three or four. Could be more. There's quite a bit of beachfront too."

"My daughter will want to see this," Sharon said, taking pictures with her phone.

They continued walking around the house until they came to an area of deep untended grass that stretched down to the water. "Is this Cape Cod Bay or the ocean?" Phyllis wondered, taking out a package of oyster crackers and swallowing a handful.

"It's Cape Cod Bay," Bella replied, sweeping her arm to the east. "Beyond those hedges, there is a pool and tennis court. Ben was a very accomplished swimmer in his youth," she sighed. "But, that was a long time ago."

"I'd like to take a peek at the courts and the pool," Grace said, swatting a black fly that was hovering around her eyes. "Then, we better go back to the house and see if Ben has shown up."

The group of five ambled around the tennis courts now overgrown with wildflowers, the poles listing, an old net, full of holes, sagging on the cracked sizzling surface.

"I'm sure Ben will be able to give us more history of the property," Bella said, as she and Grace trailed the others over to the pool.

"Yes. I'm sure he will," Grace said. A slight breeze was coming off the water now, and the early evening sky was deepening, turning shades of melon and teal. The birds were quieting down and the sea was calm. Small waves lapped the water's edge.

"Help!" someone cried. "Oh my God! Grace, come quick!"

Grace glanced at Bella, and then ran around a hedge to where Phyllis, Sharon, and Mary, screeching like a flock of angry seagulls, were charging toward them. Sharon screamed past her and Grace nearly collided with Mary, who grabbed her by both arms and cried, gasping for breath, "There's a man floating in the pool! Beyond the hedge!"

Without hesitation, Grace jumped into the pool, the sparkling water splashing over her head and swam with Bella right behind her, who moved through the water with the surprising ease and strength of a seal, to where a man floated face down in the water.

"It's Ben," Bella said, her voice wavering, as they turned him over. "He's dead," she added with a sob.

"I'm calling 911!" Mary shouted.

"Pull him over to the stairs," Grace said to Bella who, apparently in her shock and distress was treading water and staring at the sky as though expecting some sort of divine intervention. Taking hold of one arm, they propelled the nearly weightless body to the stairs and lifted it as far as they were able, and left Ben sprawled on the steps in his green striped bathing trunks. His blue eyes were wide and a dark hole, the size of a dime, was in his upper chest.

Chapter Four

Later, three of the Merry Widows, no longer merry, were huddled together on a saggy porch swing while Bella sat nearby, a blanket wrapped around her sodden shoulders, gripping the arms of a rocking chair, and staring into the distance. Grace, her jeans and shirt soaked from plunging into the pool to try to save a lifeless Ben Walwyn, leaned wearily against the post at the top of the stairs, hoping that what was left of the heat from a dying sun would soon stop her shivering.

"Do you know who that neighbor is who showed up just before the emergency people arrived?" Grace asked Bella.

"Yes, his name is Roone Seymoor. He's a customer. He had a first rate lamp cleaned recently."

"He said he heard screaming and ran right over," Grace said. "He vanished pretty quickly though. I guess I can't blame him for disappearing. It's a gruesome scene."

"That it is," Bella replied, dabbing at her eyes with the edge of the blanket.

Two emergency medical technicians were busy unloading a stretcher from an ambulance, when a Massachusetts State police vehicle arrived in a cloud of sand and pulled up next to Grace's car.

"Wait here, I'll talk to them first," Grace told Bella who started to get up.

Grace watched as Detective Andre Cruz stepped out of the car and stared for a full three seconds at her car. He shook his head, frowned, and moved toward the women on the porch as Grace descended the steps. At the same time that Emma Rice, his partner, stepped gracefully out of the car, pushing a few strands of silky hair out of her eyes.

"Grace?" Cruz said, making no attempt to hide his apparent astonishment. "What are you doing here?"

"Hey, Andre. I was hiking with the Merry Widows. Found a body." Grace tried to sound as nonchalant and calm as she could. After all, it wasn't that long ago that she first met the detective at another death scene.

"What's going on? Someone's been shot?"

"Behind those bushes," Grace told him. "It's Ben Walwyn. He's dead."

Chapter Five

That evening Grace roamed aimlessly around the front room of Pearl's. Not wanting to go home and with the faint hope that a busy mind might block out the grisly memories of the past few hours, she stopped by her shop intending to plunge into the sorting and unpacking that needed to be done before she could reopen. Normally, she would have enjoyed being alone without the daily chatter of customers and staff. But, tonight, despite the disorder of the shop and all that she had to do, she couldn't bring herself to accomplish much of anything. She brewed a cup of green tea, sorted through some boxes packed with lampshades, and tried unsuccessfully to locate her painting supplies. She soon turned off the lights, lit an oil lamp, and curled up in her Martha Washington chair, no longer shivering, but, definitely feeling unsettled after the earlier events of the day. The Merry Widows had given their statements to the police and headed home hours ago. Bella said she was shook up but would try to relax with a hot bath. Now, Grace, surrounded by the clutter of old lamps, piles of ribbons, and fabrics tried to unwind by gazing around the shop at the wide plank floors and high ceilings. She imagined for a moment, that she might be a woman of the nineteenth century, working late, feeling exhausted, and enjoying a quick rest and cup of hot tea.

A sharp knock on the door aroused her from her brief respite. She looked out her front window and saw the detective, Andre Cruz, standing on the porch. He was checking his watch when she opened the door. When he looked up, she was greeted by the unforgettable intensity of his deep green eyes.

"Working late?" he asked. "Kind of dark in here."

Andre Cruz was a detective with the Massachusetts State Police and Emma Rice was his attractive partner. The previous winter Grace and Andre started going together after they met and became embroiled in a local murder investigation. It was the first time she had found herself falling for someone since her husband, Jack, a police officer with the Barnstable Police department, had suffered a fatal heart attack while swimming at Craigville Beach.

Andre had appeared at her cottage one snowy day last winter to talk to her about the murder of a woman who lived in the village. Circumstances forced her to become involved in the investigation. It was then that she and Andre began a tentative romantic relationship that slowly evolved into one that she believed was sure and true. At least that's what she'd told herself when she wasn't obsessing jealously over his partner, Emma Rice, and her omnipresent presence.

There was undeniably lots of passion and heat in the beginning, but there were also issues that wouldn't go away. Most importantly, that Grace was jealous of Andre's relationship with Emma. Too close even for partners she thought. Andre seemed to be unsure of what he wanted and unwilling to make her feel that she wasn't imagining things going on with Emma. Finally they had gone their separate ways.

"I have so much to do, I thought I'd come here and get some things organized, but after what happened..." Grace said.

"It's nice to see you." Andre interrupted.

"You, too. You look... well..."

"Well what?"

"Good."

"Good," he repeated. "Okay... then, let's talk about today's events. No point in getting sidetracked."

"Of course," Grace said, rousing herself to the present. "What brings you to Pearl's? How did you know I was here?"

"I'm a detective." Andre smiled, his dimple visible even in the dim porch light.

"Ah, yes. I do remember that," Grace said. "Well, come in then."

Andre took in the crowded room. "You made the big move, I see. Smells like fresh paint. Lots of work to do."

Grace tried to see the store through his eyes. "It's coming together. I'm going to re-open in a few days." She removed a pile of fabrics from a dusty chair and gestured for him to have a seat. "Shouldn't you be out hunting down suspects?"

"I *am* checking out suspects."

Grace felt herself cringe. "Me? You're not serious are you?"

He shrugged. "I thought maybe you could fill me in on Ben Walwyn. We need to find out more about him, who his friends and associates were. Bella mentioned that he and Mason Crawford had an altercation when he was leaving here."

"Yes. It was a shoving match, some threats made. I don't know what they were arguing about. I recognized Mason from the courthouse and the probation department."

"I figured you would know who he is. He's been in trouble since he was a kid. But, so has Ben."

Once again, Grace was momentarily distracted as she watched Andre sweep his fingers through his thick black hair which he was wearing longer than he had when she last saw him. He was dressed in jeans and a black tee shirt, and she noticed that his olive skin, reflecting his Portuguese heritage, was summer tanned. She briefly imagined him kayaking around Cape Cod Bay shirtless, the sun beating down on his back and arms. When she realized that he was watching her, she managed to ask, "Have either of them been to State Prison?"

"Mason has. Twice, then parole, and now he's on probation again. Ben was on probation too. Your friend Audrey was his probation officer."

"Have you talked to her yet?"

"Emma interviewed her."

"Okay, good," Grace said briskly. "Is there anything else? I really should close up now. It's getting late."

"Just a couple of more things," Andre said, flipping back a page of his notebook. "Bella was a friend of Ben's mother, Imogene?"

"Yes, they were both nurses in Korea and the best of

friends. Bella's known Ben since he was born."

"Do you know why he came to see Bella today? He doesn't appear to be the type of fellow who would be frequenting a lamp shop."

"Michael said he would come by now and then and have a smoke with Bella."

"I didn't know Bella smoked? Something new?"

"No, apparently not. According to Michael, she and Ben occasionally smoked cigars. I really don't know why. Some kind of custom."

Andre looked up at her from his notebook. His eyes were bright, and he looked like he was trying to hold back a laugh. "I'm sorry," he said, "I'm having a wonderful image of Bella enjoying a stogie with such a rough looking character."

Grace felt a momentary release of tension. "We both know that Bella can be full of surprises," she agreed.

"She certainly can be," Andre said. "Okay, back to Ben's visit. Did he stay long?"

Grace remembered Andre's quicksilver nature. He had the ability to be laughing one moment, and serious the next. "I don't know. I arrived at Pearl's right before he left."

"Did you talk to him?"

"No, he seemed pretty intoxicated to me. I was glad he was on his way out," she said. Realizing that she had finished her tea and that Andre might well be thirsty, she said, "Would you like some tea? Or a beer? That's all I have, except water."

"Beer sounds good."

When she returned from the shop's kitchen, she found Andre at the front window staring out into the street. He stood in the deep shadows of the shop, barely illuminated by the faint light of the oil lamp. Grace poured the amber liquid into a glass, and joined him, hesitating for a moment, not wishing to interrupt his intense silence. She figured that he was also trying to sort through feelings that had arisen from the discovery of Ben's body. She was well aware that homicide detectives weren't immune to the pain and sadness of the discovery of a murder victim. She felt confused and suddenly shy as she stood behind him, close enough to arouse an unexpected sense of longing.

"Thanks, it's been a long, thirsty night," Andre said, taking the glass from her hand and this time, avoiding her eyes.

"Tell me about it, I feel ill every time I remember the sight of Ben, floating in the pool," Grace told him. "After we managed to pull him out of the water I checked his pulse, just to be sure, and he seemed like he was staring intently at me, even though there was no life left in him."

"Sorry, Grace. I know you had a rough day. But, even though I saw you with my own eyes, I'm having a hard time believing that you were at the scene of Ben's murder."

"Well, I didn't want to be there," she protested, suddenly feeling defensive. "You make it sound like I was there on purpose or something."

"It wasn't long ago that you were at the scene of another murder."

"I guess it *is* kind of strange, huh?"

"More than strange," Andre said. "Hopefully, you won't be involving yourself in this investigation."

"No way. I have no interest in finding out who killed Ben. I've got a shop in total disarray."

"Why were you and the other ladies at Salty Cove this evening?"

"Didn't Officer Gelb get all of the statements today? Can't you get his notes?" Grace didn't like feeling that she was being interrogated by Andre, particularly since she'd had that unpleasant experience once before.

"Okay." He closed his notebook. "I can see that my being here is making you uncomfortable. If you think of anything else, call Officer Gelb. I'm going to be out of town for a day or two."

"Gelb?" Grace knew that in Massachusetts, State Police were in charge of homicide investigations, with the support of local officers such as the young officer she had encountered during last winter's investigation. "Does he have the experience to work a homicide?"

"Everyone has to start somewhere. He might surprise you."

Although Grace thought being surprised by Gelb would be

an unlikely occurrence, she simply said, "Sharon took some photos. Has anyone checked them?"

"I'm sure someone will."

"When do you leave?"

"I'm heading for Boston tomorrow morning." André put down his beer without taking another drink. "There's a homicide conference. An instructor is ill, and I've been asked to teach some classes."

"Is Emma going too?" Grace asked, regretting it the moment the words spilled out of her mouth. How stupid could she be? "Sorry," she murmured. "I didn't mean to go there."

Andre nodded, pushed open the screen door and stepped onto the porch. "Well, I better go. Thanks for the beer." He took a final glance through the door at the messy and disorganized room. As the words that she wanted to say caught in her throat, there was silence between them. He turned, and in a moment, vanished into the night, leaving her with only the faint echo of "*Boa noite,*" as he reached the sidewalk.

Chapter Six

Grace opened her eyes to find that she was dangerously close to falling out of bed, in large part because Clambake, her black and white cat, was nestled at her side, taking up a vast amount of bed space and snoring sweetly. Gray, early morning light filtered through her bedroom curtains. It had been a humid, soggy, night, more typical of mid-summer, and she'd spent the night flailing and thrashing in her bed.

Reaching down, she laid a gentle hand on her sleeping cat. He twitched, but his snoring continued and was echoed by the rumble of thunderheads. Rain, intermittent during the night was now steady and it would have been a good morning to roll over and catch some extra sleep. Instead, Grace found herself thinking about Ben Walwyn. Those eyes of his, appeared to stare directly at her. Imploring her? To do what?

She was curious about his relationship with Bella. There was her friendship with Imogene, and he was her son, but Bella never mentioned anything specific about Imogene's family. She had never met Ben and was surprised when Michael said he was an occasional visitor to Pearl's. Although Andre had joked about Bella sharing a cigar with rough company, it did seem odd to her. Ben seemed like a troubled sort.

Excited voices followed by an insistent screech roused her from her daydreams. Moving her curtains aside she looked out at the foggy, opalescent marsh. Dark clouds drifted above Cape Cod Bay and hovered close to the dunes on Sandy Neck, a barrier beach that separated the harbor from Cape Cod Bay. An easterly wind was blowing strong and white caps churned a metallic gray. Marsh grass bowed down to the wind and swept mud in tiny rivulets toward her cottage.

The Great Marsh lapped the edge of her yard barely thirty feet from her back door. Spartina, eel and turtle grasses thrived in the sand and mudflats. All manner of wild life including; clams, crabs, and barnacles flourished in the mud. Whimbrels, sand pipers, snowy plovers and green herons flew above the sandy soil and grass. An osprey nest, atop a repurposed telephone pole, perched like a flag above the marshland. She knew that it would soon be time for the resident ospreys to leave for their long vacation someplace warm and sunny, like Cuba or South America, only to return in March and nest atop the pole in their house of sticks and marsh leavings. All in all, the marsh was alive with activity, including the occasional raccoon that emerged onto Grace's lawn for a poke around her garbage cans.

Grace was startled to see two men in hooded windbreakers, hurrying across the marsh carrying a ladder and stepping carefully on wooden pilings that formed a bridge of sorts. Staring through a pair of binoculars she kept handy on her bedside table, she focused on the unfolding scene.

"Clambake, I think those guys are running out to our Osprey nest. Uh oh! There's a bird dangling from it. I better get dressed and find out what's going on."

Grace ran across her damp lawn, the stiff, moist breeze working against her. Goldfinches chattered in the tree branches, reminding her that their feeder socks were empty. Ignoring them, she cautiously managed to weave her way avoiding deep rills and cracks, along the familiar marsh trail, where she joined one of the men now standing under the untidy nest.

"Can I help?" she asked, before she realized that it was Mason Crawford. His hair, an unruly mass of gray and brown, protruded from underneath his hood. She had last seen him in front of Pearl's a few hours before Ben was killed.

"I was driving by with my boss," Mason told her. "He told me to stop. There's a problem in the bird nest."

Grace followed his gaze upwards. At the top of the ladder peering into the nest, was none other than Roone Seymoor, the neighbor who arrived at Salty Cove shortly after Ben's body was discovered. An osprey dangled over the edge, flapped enormous wings, and pecked at something wrapped around one of its legs.

"I called the Cape Wildlife Center and the Long Pasture Wildlife Sanctuary," Grace said. "Someone will be out to help." Wind whipped her chestnut hair into her eyes. She tucked a few strands behind her ears. "Those are my ospreys. I've adopted them."

"Looks like this one's caught up in some kind of rope or twine," Roone said, leaning against the ladder, and adjusting his gloves as the pole shifted an inch or two. "You wouldn't believe how big this nest is and what a load of stuff is in it. There's a bunch of fishing wire, a stuffed animal and what looks like part of an oar. I've got some wire clippers. If he'll let me, I'll try to untie him. What do you want me to do?"

Well, I'm not sure," Grace said. "We don't want to traumatize the poor bird any more than we have to, but maybe you should... Gosh, I don't really know what we should do."

"So much for *your* ospreys," he muttered.

"Look," Mason said, pointing in the direction of Freezer Road. "It must be those bird experts."

Grace sighed with relief as two twenty-something's, who looked like they might be brother and sister, arrived and identified themselves as Alexis and Rick. Since Roone was already atop the ladder with gloves and clippers, the bird rescuers decided it would be best for him to clip the twine. Roone spoke soothingly to the agitated bird, and then with one smooth motion, he freed it, and placed it back into the nest.

"Okay. We'll take it from here." Alexis said, pulling the hood of her rain jacket over her head as a dark cloud passed.

Roone climbed down the ladder. "We meet again," he said to Grace.

"Yes," Grace said, noticing the striking hazel eyes in the equally striking, handsome face.

"Terrible business out at Salty Cove," Roone said.

"Horrible," Grace agreed.

Roone nodded, and perhaps not knowing what else to say, he changed the subject back to the present. "Mason does occasional gardening for me. We were buying plants and stopped for breakfast at the wharf. We were heading back to my place when I spotted the osprey in obvious distress. Hope he'll be all right."

"Me too," Grace said. "Actually, I think it's a she. It's very hard to tell the difference unless you watch them carefully. But, I do think this is probably the female. She's got speckles on her chest."

"So you *do* know something about ospreys."

"I know that they're scavengers and like to pile things in their nests," she said. "I'd love to have a look up there myself."

"That nest is huge," he replied. "Must weigh a hundred pounds, maybe more. Unfortunately, it has a lot of plastic and other garbage, like the twine that wrapped his, I mean her leg. I guess we both learned something new today."

There was, Grace thought, a lot to learn about a number of things, the contents of the nest, being the least of them.

Chapter Seven

Reluctant to leave her osprey, but recognizing that the bird was in good hands, Grace hiked the remaining distance through the wet marsh to her cottage, her flip-flops soaked with muck, squeaking with every step. The wind, warm and humid, crept up under her wet cotton shirt, causing her to shudder. Pulling it off as she stepped into her kitchen, she threw it on the back of a chair to collect later, and was filling a glass of ice with cold water when she heard a knock at her front door.

Peeking around the stairwell so that she could see the front door unobserved, she saw Andre Cruz on her porch. And so was his partner, Emma Rice.

"What now?" Grace mumbled. Maybe she should just ignore them. After all, she was muddy, sweaty and half undressed. Not the way she wanted to appear in front of either of them.

There was another knock. "Oh, for heaven's sake. I'm coming, just a minute," she called out, fumbling with the buttons of her damp shirt before opening the door.

"I left some papers here," Andre said, without so much as hello.

"Here?" Grace said to Andre's back as he headed for the kitchen. What was he talking about she wondered. He hadn't been to her house in months.

"Hey, Grace," Emma said. "Have you recovered from discovering another dead body?"

Grace noted the sarcasm. As if Emma would care about how she felt. She knew that she just wanted to ridicule her, as she was heading off to Boston with Andre. At least, Grace supposed she was. Andre hadn't actually answered her question the night before.

"I have," she replied as evenly as possible.

"Good for you," Emma said. "By the way, there's something wrong with your shirt."

Grace looked down and saw that her buttons had found their way to the wrong buttonholes, leaving her shirt cockeyed, and Grace feeling like a five year old.

"Oh. I was just out in the marsh, and I was in a hurry, and..."

"Thanks. Sorry to bother you," Andre interrupted as he swept past her and joined Emma on the porch.

That was more than strange, Grace thought as Andre drove off. Was he conducting a quick search of her house? She was also alarmed and surprised at her reaction to Emma. Her heart sank. It was as if she were still in love with Andre. She found herself wishing that Emma had chosen a career as a swimsuit model or just about anything else, instead of joining the Massachusetts State Police force. Grace had heard all about partnerships and cop 'marriages.' Her husband, Jack, had explained how bonds were formed out of necessity. It was supposed to be a good thing, after all, safety first. Andre and Emma were definitely bonded.

Jack, a sunny outgoing man, had known he wanted to be a police officer when he was five years old. Andre, on the other hand, had told her he became an officer out of necessity, a newly married man who needed a career. His marriage didn't last, but his commitment to his job never wavered. And, Grace thought, it suited him. It was an outlet for his creative, masculine energy. Andre was a deeper, darker personality than Jack. Things were never easy with him. If Jack was joy and sunlight, Andre was complexity and twilight.

Grace poured herself a cup of coffee. She reflected on her feelings of jealousy. She acknowledged that she might have felt a bit envious of Emma, but she was much better now than she had been when she was dating Andre. As she lifted the cup to her lips, she noticed a scrap of paper stuck to the bottom. She put the mug down, splashing coffee on the counter. "What the...?" she asked aloud.

"Gracie," the note said. "I've missed you."

Chapter Eight

Although it was now mid-morning, the day was dark, and rain beat about Grace as she darted across the street to Pearl's. She enjoyed walking in the heavy shower, particularly after the intense heat of the past few days. Besides, she'd already been soaked to the skin after running around the marsh helping to rescue her osprey.

A horn blared, and a dark blue sedan slammed to a stop, a few inches from Grace, who startled, dropped her umbrella and the bag that was tucked under her arm. There was the distinctive sound of glass smashing as her bag hit the pavement.

A woman, with silver hair cut in last year's fashionable spiky short style, glared at her through her wet windshield.

Grace picked up her bag, and as she approached the driver, she heard her say to her passenger, "It *is* a problem! I know what he said. But I know it was there before she died and now it's gone missing. Now they're both dead."

Leaning out her window, she said to Grace, "Damn it! Why don't you watch where you're going?"

"Can't you see I'm in a crosswalk? You made me drop my lamp, and it's shattered. What's the matter with you?"

When the woman rolled up her window and beeped her horn again, Grace stepped in front of the car. She retrieved her umbrella and folded her arms across her chest, at which point, the passenger door flew open. A tall man with a shock of woolly white hair, wearing a navy blue suit, stepped out of the vehicle and approached Grace with a look of impatience.

"Look, we're sorry about you lamp. What did it cost you?" He opened his wallet.

"It's not mine actually, and not expensive. I think it was worth about twenty dollars."

"Will that do?" The man handed Grace two twenties. Not waiting for a reply, he got back in the car, which lurched forward as Grace moved to the safety of the sidewalk.

"Someone's in a big hurry." Grace turned at the sound of a familiar voice to find Clay Davenport, a local decorator, standing next to her on the sidewalk. "You do manage to get yourself into the strangest predicaments. But I see you scored a bit of cash on that maneuver." Clay held a huge black umbrella over her head as they crossed the street.

"I didn't maneuver anything and that wasn't a 'score,' Grace protested. "The man graciously offered to pay for the lamp, and that was that."

"Well, you did make a few bucks now, didn't you?" Clay responded. "And what kind of lamp were you carrying anyway? Must have been something rather chintzy, given the value you placed on it."

Grace stepped onto Pearl's front porch. "Sorry, Clay. It was that lamp you bought at a garage sale. You said you paid twenty dollars for it. I took it home to make a shade for it."

Clay shook water from his plaid trench coat before tossing it on the wicker settee by Pearl's front door. "Are you serious? I said twenty? Not two hundred? Really, Grace, I think you owe me for this mistake of yours."

Grace stared at Clay, taking in his tall thin frame, his hair, this week, a tousled gray with white highlights, and his beady bird-like eyes and thought, how odd it was she had never noticed how much he looked like an osprey. A very snooty and annoying osprey who might well entangle himself in anything that came along.

Chapter Nine

As they entered the shop, Grace shoved her umbrella in the stand by the door. Clay hung on to his, dripping across the floor as he called out to Michael who popped up from behind an art nouveau floor lamp.

"What in heaven's name is that odd piece of art you're hiding behind?" Clay asked.

Michael pushed his round glasses higher on his nose. "It belongs to a customer by the name of Roone Seymoor. It may look strange, but it's quite an unusual and valuable lamp."

"That's a coincidence," Grace said. "I just saw him this morning. An osprey got tangled in some rope, and Roone and his gardener, Mason Crawford, came to the rescue."

"Mason Crawford and Roone Seymoor?" Michael asked. "That *is* a strange duo."

Clay circled the lamp. "It's rather curious isn't it? But, I do like that arrow design on the arm. I wonder if this Roone fellow might wish to sell? I might have the perfect customer for such a piece."

"I doubt it. Mr.Seymoor rarely sells any of his collection of fine lamps," Michael said, taking Clay's umbrella, depositing it in the stand, and wiping the wet floor with paper towels. "Really, Clay, can't you be more careful? What if a customer slipped and fell? We'd all be sued."

"Well, not me, of course." Clay said. "But speaking of suing and such things, Grace broke that lovely lamp I brought in last week. It shattered on the sidewalk right in front of my eyes. I spent a lot of money on it and I'll be expecting reimbursement."

"You mean the little glass lamp you got at the garage sale?

Michael asked. "That wasn't worth the twenty you said you paid for it."

"Hush, Michael." Clay held out his hand. "Give me the forty, Grace, and we'll call it a day."

Grace was well aware that Clay could be a total nuisance, and knowing that she didn't have patience for his selfish behavior, placed the two twenties into his greedy palm. "There. Settled?"

Clay shrugged. "You should have held out for more. That was Trevor and Portia Spear in the Mercedes. They're loaded. I've been trying to get them to hire me as their decorator, but it seems that they are loyal to some woman from Boston. Can you believe it?"

Grace didn't know about Trevor and Portia, but she knew that loyalty would be a novel idea for Clay. He was a talented decorator and designer, but he was a gossip who often dished the dirt on his clients without so much as a blush.

"Grace, have you seen Clay's new business card?" Michael asked with a smile.

"Oh, yes. Here, you must have a look. I designed it myself, and I must say I think it's fabulous."

Grace accepted the silver metallic card from Clay's manicured fingers. The font was in old English script, chartreuse highlighted with black. The card announced Clay's services as a decorator to the stars as well as unnamed locals of prestigious pedigree. Grace tried her best not to burst out laughing. She didn't dare look at Michael who was barely containing himself while dusting a pleated lampshade with considerable attention.

"I didn't know we had many stars here on the Cape," Grace said.

Frowning, Clay snatched back the card. "There *are* stars here on the Cape and many famous people as you know. What I'm referring to is my years in Hollywood. I was quite in demand."

"When were you in California? I had no idea."

"About thirty years ago. I met many of the most famous people at the most wonderful parties." Clay gazed off in the distance and casually dropped his card behind a table lamp.

Amused, Grace was reminded that Clay dropped his card everywhere he could. She'd found it in books at the library, stuffed into the sugar packet containers in restaurants and on theatre seats. He certainly had no qualms about self-promotion.

"You could use some excitement around here," Clay continued. "It's about time you scheduled an opening party to celebrate your move."

Grace sighed. Her day was going downhill fast. Beginning with the helpless osprey, then a visit from Andre and Emma, followed by a near accident, a broken lamp, and now, Clay Davenport, at his most charming self.

Michael quickly intervened, possibly having stopped Grace from committing a homicide of her own and steered Clay down the hall to the kitchen, with the promise of free food.

"You've got some of your homemade brownies?" Grace heard him say as she retrieved his card and tucked it in her pocket. "Why, Michael, how sweet of you. How thoughtless of Grace not to mention them."

As Clay meandered toward the tiny kitchen, he bumped into a stack of shades. As Grace settled the quivering pile, and reflected on Clay's self-absorption, she remembered all of the narcissists, personality disorders, psychopaths and other assorted deviants that she dealt with on a daily basis in her previous career. It was a little more than a year ago, that she had decided to make a monumental career shift, by quitting her job as a probation officer and purchasing Pearl's Antique Lamps and Shades. She'd been browsing in Beau's Books one day during her lunch break, when the previous owners of Pearl's, Matt and Milo, came to say goodbye to him. The lamp shop was for sale, and although they hadn't had a serious offer, they were anxious to get settled in their retirement home and were leaving for Jacksonville, Florida within a few days. When Grace showed the slightest bit of interest, which she believed was just a polite kind of interest, the two men, who she later affectionately dubbed M& M, made her what seemed to be a fair and enticing offer on the spot. When she mumbled something about her lack of any expertise in the lamp business, they had excitedly convinced her that they would be happy to guide her along, albeit from Jacksonville. They were, they said, very confident it would be an easy transition for her and when she told them she'd studied art in college and painted the occasional watercolor, they were very enthusiastic about her ability to learn to paint lampshades. Nothing to it, they assured her.

She went home, spent a restless night pacing the floors of her cottage, sitting down now and then to make notes and figure out some financial calculations. By morning, utterly exhausted, but excited, she decided to take the plunge. She had often dreamed of owning her own store, and Pearl's seemed like just the life change she needed. She signed the papers with M&M the following day.

Then, last winter, Beau approached her with the suggestion that they switch places in the nineteenth century house on Main Street that housed Pearl's and his bookstore, Beau's Books. Beau was barely able to eke out a living from his shop, but he wasn't ready to give up. He wanted to make his store into a bookstore specifically dedicated to Cape Cod's history, architecture, people, and poetry, "everything Cape Cod" as he described it. He figured that he could save money on rent, by moving upstairs, where, in addition to the shop space, there was a large loft area, where he could store boxes for shipping and surplus stock. He was, he promised Grace, quite willing to live peacefully with the mice that resided there.

It had only taken a few minutes for Grace to agree to the idea. Her two shop assistants, Michael and Bella, were getting on in years. It would make it so much easier on them if they didn't have to climb stairs to the upper floor. And, no doubt, she needed the two of them, Bella with her skills wiring, repairing and cleaning lamps, as well as her remarkable expertise in antique lighting and Michael's extraordinary skill as a salesman. She had come to depend on them greatly.

Furthermore, she was excited that Pearl's would have a street side location with windows at eye level, full of displays of beautiful lamps, and facing onto a cozy front porch, a location that would be sure to entice more customers into her store.

"It looks very nice in here," Grace said to Michael when he returned from the kitchen. "You and Duane have made a lot of progress since yesterday."

"What did you expect? While you and the Merry Widows were out gallivanting around the countryside, discovering dead bodies and such, I've been toiling away in here," Michael said. "Can't say the same for Duane though. He's been here, but not exactly toiling, if you know what I mean."

Duane, clumsy and awkward, was a challenge for all of them, but particularly for Michael, who was easily upset by days that lacked comfortable routines. Last December, Grace hired Duane for what was supposed to be a few weeks around the holidays, well aware that he'd had problems with drugs and at age nineteen, was residing at Pinewood, the local rehab center, as a condition of probation. Still, knowing that people with criminal records had a hard time finding work, she agreed to take him on as a temporary employee. And then, after the holidays were over, realizing she needed someone young and strong, she offered him a full-time job. Besides, she liked Duane. He was doing his best to learn the ropes and showed up more or less on time each day.

The sharp bang of the front door announced the arrival of Sophie, a plump nine-year-old girl, carrying a gray and white striped cat. The squirming ball of fur sported a bright red leash, which precisely matched Sophie's sneakers.

"Hi, Grace. Hi, Michael," she said, dropping her wet umbrella on the floor. "I was taking Stanley for a walk when I thought I'd drop by and say hello."

She placed Stanley gingerly on the floor, and patted him on the head. Michael ran to get more paper towels.

Sophie was the daughter of the owners of the Beach Sparrow Inn and Tea Room, housed in a lovely colonial, a short walk from Pearl's. An independent soul, she liked to wander around the village and visit the various shops and businesses. Everyone kept an eye out for her, because she frequently neglected to tell her parents that she had left the inn.

"Hey, Sophie," Grace greeted her. "Do your parents know

where you are?"

"Of course they do. Why is everybody always asking me that question?" Sophie rolled her eyes and presented them with an exaggerated smile.

"Because you frequently go missing," Michael said, reaching down to grab Stanley, who was in position to leap on a table of delicate lamps, and placed him back in her arms. "There are brownies in the kitchen. Clay's down there. Why don't you go say hello."

Grace smiled. Of course, one of the main reasons that Sophie visited was because she knew that, thanks to Michael, there was always something sweet to eat in Pearl's small kitchen. In fact, Pearl's had become somewhat of a local hangout. There were a number of local eateries, but folks from the neighborhood often stopped by to check in with Michael and Bella, both longtime residents of the village, to chat and pass time between errands, and share a cup of coffee and sample a brownie or two. Michael was happy to see everyone and obviously enjoyed his reputation as an amateur baker. Bella was always ready to lend an ear to anyone who had troubles or wanted to share a secret. Of course, some folks came to see Grace as well, but she was under no illusions as to who were the important people at Pearl's.

"So you heard about Ben Walwyn?" Grace said, now that she was alone with Michael.

"It's all over town." Michael lowered his voice. "The folks I've talked to were horrified by the murder, but not terribly surprised that someone killed him. He was known as a troublemaker." Dipping a brush in a quart of paint, he smacked it expertly on the edge of the can. "It is unsettling that he was in here visiting Bella, just hours before he went to meet his maker."

The shop door banged shut again as Bella was propelled swiftly into the shop on a strong current of air.

"The wind is picking up, and it's just ghastly out there," she announced, peeling off her raincoat and kicking off her sneakers. "I left my umbrella on the porch to dry out, but we better keep an eye on it or it will be doing a Mary Poppins all over town. Now, where did I leave my slippers?" she asked.

"I heard you and the Merry Widows had a bit of a surprise yesterday, Bella."

"Michael!" Grace said.

"Sorry to hear about your friend," Michael said.

Bella heaved a great sigh. "Yes, it is a tragedy. His mother was my very best friend." Tears formed in her eyes. After a moment, she wiped them away and then gazed around the room. "Has Duane brought my tools down yet?"

"Hi, Ms. Bella," Duane said, as he drifted in, head bent over his phone, fingers busy sending a text message. "I sure did. I put them in your new work area."

"Thank you, Duane. I need to get to work. I didn't sleep too well, as you might imagine."

"I *can* imagine," Duane said. "Remember when I found the body of ...?"

"Oh yes, well, never mind," Bella interrupted him. "Bad as things may be, we can't let every damn thing keep us from our work, now can we?"

"Wow, Ms. Bella. I never heard you talk like that before."

"I was a Captain in the U.S. Army Corps of Nurses! I've heard far worse words than that, for goodness sakes," she declared. "But, in any case, I meant to say darn. That other word, slipped out before I knew it."

"Wow, Ms. Bella. I mean Captain Bella."

"Bella will do just fine, Duane."

Grace followed Bella to the area where she would repair, polish, and work her magic on all manner of odd objects folks brought in to be made into lamps. There were the usual models, toy boats, lighthouses, and ships. And there were plenty of the unusual, such as a license plate, a boot, and a trophy for synchronized swimming. "Michael can be insensitive at times," Grace said. "I'm sure he didn't mean to be rude."

"No, of course not. I'm used to Michael. And, he is adorable in a cranky kind of way."

"Need some help setting up your tools?" Grace asked.

"As you know, I have my own way of doing things, but if you would give me a hand with the heavier stuff, I'll do the deciding where things should go. And, I want to talk to you some more about what happened yesterday. And speaking of not sleeping, you don't look so good yourself, I might add."

"Not a great day so far. I've been running around in the rain, helping to rescue my osprey. And ..."

"What is it, Grace?"

"Nothing," she fibbed.

"Can't fool me," Bella said.

"Andre came by last night to talk to me about the murder," Grace said, knowing from past experience that there was no use trying to deceive Bella. "He'll be working the case, but he's on his way to a conference in Boston for a couple of days."

"Andre? Well, perhaps you'll feel like telling me more about him some other time," Bella said, arching her eyebrows.

Grace nodded. She knew that Bella was a keen observer of the fluctuating moods of those around her. She was a kind, sensitive person, and most likely recognized that Grace wasn't ready to talk to her about Andre yet.

"I'm glad you felt up to coming to work," Grace said. "Yesterday was an awful shock. I hope Phyllis, Sharon, and Mary are all okay."

"I talked to all of them this morning. They're upset of course. Finding a dead man is not the norm for our walks."

"No, of course not. Tell me more about Imogene and Ben. You mentioned that you and she were in Korea together."

"Yes. We were very close. I don't have anyone else to talk to about the war, and sometimes I wish I did," she shuddered. "It was a long time ago, but one does not forget."

Grace put a hand on Bella's shoulder and waited for her to continue her story in her own way.

"I'll tell you more about Imogene as we work." Bella rubbed her hand along a counter top and held her palm out. "It's been dusted! I see Michael couldn't resist tidying up my space."

Grace looked at the neatly stacked boxes. Definitely, not Duane's' work, she thought, as Bella started pulling sockets, cords, and switches out of cartons.

"Imogene was a bit of an eccentric," Bella continued. "She

had her faults, just like most of us, but deep down where it counts, she was the best friend anyone could have. We helped each other out of many a scrape in Korea and I felt that I owe her mightily. I promised her I would stay in touch with the children. She was always worried about Ben. He certainly was the cutest, most delightful boy."

"Did he have a difficult life?" Grace asked, recalling the rough looking man she'd met.

"Well, no," Bella said, apparently reading her thoughts. "I'm speaking of a long time ago. Ben was not the man he once was."

Pulling packing tape off of a carton, she ripped it open and began lining up smaller boxes of various types of screws, bolts, and connectors on a temporary sawhorse bench. "I'm not sure what went wrong. Imogene was always there for him. She spent a lot of time helping him with his lessons. Even so, he barely made it through high school, but he was very popular because he was athletic and very good-looking. In any case, the girls seemed to like him."

Taking a deep breath she leaned against her counter. "Are you sure I can put these things away, Grace?' The construction people won't mess with them?"

"No, they said they're done in this area. A few more days and everything will be finished."

"All right, where was I?" Bella continued "William, the oldest of Imogene's kids, is a successful defense attorney."

"I know who he is," Grace said." I've met him a few times when I used to work at the courthouse."

"He's married to Morgan. She's a lawyer too, and they have a couple of boys away at college. He's very nice. Very smart. Went to Harvard, I think."

"Uh huh. The successful son and the wayward son. Classic."

Their sister Portia is married to Trevor Spear. I'm not sure exactly what he does. Financial advisor or something of that sort. Ben always lived at home with Imogene."

Grace recalled her encounter with the couple in the Mercedes. The woman didn't appear to be particularly sad about her brother's demise, but then, everyone grieves in his or her own way. Weren't grief and anger, often, different sides of the same coin?

"You mentioned yesterday that he was an accomplished swimmer."

"Yes. He was good at sailing, tennis, archery, just about any sport he tried. A natural athlete. He was once considered for the US Olympic swim team, but he didn't make the final cut."

"No kidding?" Grace lugged a heavy carton over to Bella." That's quite an accomplishment."

"Yes, it was. Later, he had a good business giving swimming and archery lessons to the sea scouts and anyone else who was interested. But, eventually, alcohol got the better of him. Prospective clientele stayed away. Obviously, parents didn't want their children learning swimming and archery from someone with a drinking problem. Besides, he started to run with a rough crowd." Bella hesitated, perhaps remembering the troubled Ben, or maybe the younger more charismatic child. "But murdered? The poor man. I wish I knew what happened. Did I mention that he was my godson?"

"I didn't know. I'm so sorry Bella. Whatever problems he may have had, it's a terrible thing to have to cope with," Grace said.

Bella reached over and grabbed Grace's arm. "You have to help me find out who murdered him."

"Oh, Bella, I can't. I'm not an investigator and I have enough problems here at the shop."

"Speaking of problems," Michael piped up as Duane tripped in.

"Is it okay if I bring down the rest of the lamps?" Duane asked. "Beau says he's up to his ears in books and lamps."

Moving the boxes of lamps from the old upstairs Pearl's, and out of harm's way, during the construction phase had been a daunting task. Beau let her leave many of the lamps upstairs, at least until now, and she was stumbling over cartons and boxes at her own house. Michael and Bella absorbed about as much as they could handle, and were more than ready to get the lamps back to Pearl's. Duane had been charged with the task of moving and storing the lamps during the renovation. That included finding lamps that customers were coming around to pick up after a repair, or a lampshade that had been hand painted by Grace. Duane said he had a 'system', and could find anything at a moment's notice. Unfortunately, Duane's notion of systems and 'a moment's notice' were unlike anyone else's. It often took him hours, driving around to Michael's, Bella's, and Grace's houses, to find anything.

"Yes. Beau has been more than patient. Just stack whatever is left, wherever you can find room. Use the kitchen if you have to," Grace said apologetically. "Then, when the final repairs are done, we'll move everything back and set up."

"Yup, got it. No problem, Ms. Tolliver," Duane said just as the bell on the door jangled, announcing the arrival of yet another visitor who had chosen to ignore the 'closed' sign on the front door.

Michael had hung the bell earlier this morning. "For security purposes," he'd said.

"Bella? You here?"

"Now, who's that?" Bella replied.

"It's me, William." A sturdy gray haired, goateed, middle-aged man in a tan suit, white shirt and burgundy tie, wove his way among the lamps, pausing briefly to stare at the art nouveau lamp with the arrow. "Peculiar," he muttered, wiping raindrops out of his hair.

"William!" Bella stepped over a pile of lamp parts and wrapped her arms around the man. "It's so good to see you. How are you holding up?"

"I don't think I'll ever get over this. The police told me that you found Ben's body. That must have been awful for you."

"Yes, of course it was," Bella said. "Excuse me. I don't think you've met Grace Tolliver. She bought the shop last year. I do believe you've met Michael Shipworth, and this is Duane Kerbey, our young colleague.

Clay wandered back into the room, munching on a brownie, while Sophie with her cat, Stanley, straggled behind him. When

Bella introduced Clay to William, he wiped off his fingers with a napkin, and then stashed it behind an onion bottle lamp. Clearly appalled, Michael seized Clay by the elbow as he started to sit down in the comfy Martha Washington chair, recently recovered in yellow chintz, and steered him in the direction of the front door, and at the same time, signaling to Sophie that it was time she was on her way as well.

William hovered a moment, before heaving himself into the chair, letting out a deep sigh. Bella, plopped herself down on her work stool. A few lamps perched on glass shelves rattled as the door slammed signaling Clay and Sophie's enforced departure.

"I've just got a few minutes before I'm due back in court," William announced, taking a quick glance at his phone. "Mother would have been so upset. I'm glad she's not around to see this. She couldn't bear it. Ben was her favorite, of course. Everyone knew that."

Bella reached out and patted the man's knee. "Imogene loved you all the same. In fact, she adored you and Portia. But, Ben needed so much of her attention."

"Ben was certainly an attention getter. That's for sure."

"Imogene told me that you represented him in court and helped him out financially. She appreciated all you did."

"Portia and Trevor helped out too. We're all family."

"Were you aware that Ben stopped by here yesterday?" Bella asked William. "I'm grateful that I had a chance to have a chat with him. He was full of future plans and hinted that he was involved in a happy romantic relationship. When I mentioned that I was going walking with my friends, he invited us out to tour the property. That's why we happened to be out there last evening. Before he left here, he told me that Imogene left the estate to him and that he was going to get married, fix up the house and open a B&B."

"That's right. Mom left him Salty Cove. She left some money for Portia and me, but I guess she thought that Ben would need a home. It's hard to imagine how Ben would operate a B&B when he was incapable of taking care of himself. "

"I can only guess that she was worried about him. Poor

Ben."

"I'm sure my mother had the best intentions, but Ben was a grown man," William said. "I think she should have shown him the door years ago."

"I suspect he kept her company. I can imagine that it might have been rather frightening to live in that huge house alone," Bella said in a flat tone, but Grace thought she looked uncomfortable with William's critical comment about his recently departed mother and brother.

"I guess you're right," William said, pulling himself out of the plushy chair with a grunt. "However, I do believe she should have divided everything up three ways. That would have been the fairest and simplest thing to do. She did leave Portia and I a bit more in the way of investments, which was, I suppose, her way of compensating, but with the economic downturn, they aren't worth anywhere near what they were a few years ago. Now, I suppose Portia and I will inherit Salty Cove. We'll need to discuss what to do with the property soon. I'd love to keep it, and I'm sure Portia would, too, but we both have houses on the Cape already.

How eager he was to move on, Grace thought. Didn't he realize that now was a time to grieve for Ben?

Chapter Ten

Tony Bennett's smooth voice drifted through the screen door on Thomas De Pace's back porch as Grace stepped through the back hallway that led to her father's kitchen. Spaghetti sauce was bubbling over the edge of a skillet, leaving red splotches on the white cook top, and a pot of water was boiling over, spewing hot water at the wall. Two place settings were on the table, two wine glasses nearby. An unlit candle, leaning precariously from a fish shaped candlestick, completed the still life.

Grace started toward the living room, and was about to announce herself, when she caught a glimpse of her father, holding Gink, the young woman he hired last winter as a live-in companion, dancing by the open door. When they noticed her, they started laughing and came to a stumbling stop.

"Hi, Gracie! We're dancing!" her father said, as Gink laughed.

"I see that," Grace said as nonchalantly as she could, considering her surprise.

"I'm teaching Gink how to foxtrot. She's teaching me how to make spaghetti bolognese."

"The bolognese is bubbling over top of the pan," Grace said.

"Oh!" Gink ran toward the kitchen, with Grace and her father close behind.

"It's my fault," Thomas said, "I rather insisted on that last number. Water sure boils fast these days doesn't it?"

"No problem," Gink said. "It's pretty hard to ruin spaghetti. Are you going to join us, Grace. I've made plenty."

"Sure. I guess I will." The deep aroma of basil, garlic, and tomato sauce was making her stomach rumble.

"Gink makes darn good spaghetti," Thomas said.

Her father brought plates to the table, while Grace finished cutting a few pieces of bread. Placing a glass in front of Grace, Gink poured her and her father some wine and a glass of water for herself.

"We heard about the murder at Salty Cove," Thomas said. "We also heard that you and Bella discovered Ben Walwyn's body."

Grace described, as briefly as possible, the events of the previous day.

"I grew up a few houses away from Salty Cove," Gink said. "I knew his mother, and William and Portia, too."

Surprised by this, Grace put down her fork, and prepared to listen closely. Gink hadn't told her much about herself. All she knew was that Gink had grown up on the Cape, didn't want anything to do with her family and preferred that no one ask her too many questions. She was Duane's friend and Grace's father had met her last winter at a gathering at Pearl's after the Village Holiday Stroll. Having hastily decided Gink would make the perfect live-in caretaker and occasional driver, her father had offered Gink a place to live. In exchange, she would cook and clean for him. A generous stipend was included in his offer. Grace was grateful her father had finally admitted that he needed a live in helper. She had been a bit apprehensive at first, because she knew that Gink used to have a serious problem with alcohol and had been in rehab with Duane, but her father insisted it was Gink or no one. To Grace's relief, Gink turned out to be a wonderful companion to her Dad, despite the more than fifty years age difference.

Her father was in pretty good health but he had the type of personality that only could be described as that of risk taker. He was always involved in what seemed to Grace to be crazy schemes, which, to him seemed perfectly rational. Before he met Gink last winter, he had had an accident with a bread truck and set fire to his back porch, while barbequing a steak during a snowstorm. Since Gink arrived, Grace was able to worry less about her dad and know that there was someone in the house with him.

Grace didn't even know how she got the name Gink, and didn't want to ask her. She tried to find out more from Duane, but he didn't know much either. That she grew up in the well-to-do neighborhood near Salty Cove was a surprising bit of information.

"Imogene was such a sweetheart," Gink continued. "Whenever I ran away from home, I went to the big house, and she'd give me tea and marshmallows until my parents came and got me. Ben, William, and Portia are older than me, but Ben never left home, so I knew him better than the other two. I met up with William later." Gink looked down at her plate. "He represented me in court a couple of times. You know, when I got in trouble. He didn't even charge me."

"What about Ben?" Grace asked, hoping the revealing conversation would continue. "What was he like?"

"He was all right, I guess. My mother made me take swimming and archery lessons from him. I think she wanted to get me out of the house and out of her sight." Gink made a scornful face, leaving Grace to wonder if it was a reflection on her mother or on Ben. "He wasn't the best teacher. I mean, I did learn to swim, but for the most part I taught myself, while he worked on his tan, or drank beer with his pal Mason. I got pretty good at archery. Maybe I'll take it up again. I could use some fresh air and exercise."

"Me too!" Thomas said. "I could easily set up a range in the yard. I might even have some old arrows and a bow in the shed out back. I'll check into it first thing in the morning."

Grace groaned aloud. She was sure the thought of her dad shooting arrows in his backyard sent her already too high blood pressure a bit higher.

"Mason Crawford?" Grace asked, remembering Mason, the man that had argued with Ben in front of Pearl's and was with Roone Seymoor when he rescued the osprey.

"The very same," Gink replied, with a tone of disgust that surprised Grace. "Now there's a total loser. He and Ben were childhood friends. They both had short fuses, and often got into fights. When they got older, they often fought over a woman named Freesia Foster."

Grace mulled over this new information. She happened to know Freesia, she had been her probation officer, a few years ago when Freesia was on probation for theft, assault, and disorderly conduct. She wondered if Freesia was the reason for the argument she witnessed in front of Pearl's, hours before she and the Merry Widows discovered Ben in the pool at Salty Cove.

Grace's father's chair scraped against the floor as he pushed back from the table. "Anyone want anymore? I'm through."

Gink got up. "Grace?"

"No, thanks," Grace said, recognizing that the chance to learn more about Gink was gone.

She cleared the table, but Gink insisted on finishing up the dishes herself. Grace kissed her father goodbye. "Night, Dad," she said, adding a hug. "Keep up with those cooking and dancing lessons."

"I plan to, Gracie, as long as Gink is willing."

Grace closed the screen door and lingered on the porch where she had spent so much time as a child, sitting and dreaming on these very stairs. Although there was a lingering pinkish tint to the evening sky, a few dozen stars were visible. The air smelled of honeysuckle. Crickets chirped. She was reveling in her moment of nostalgia when, heading back to her car, she glanced at the kitchen window. She stopped in her tracks. Gink was standing over the sink and sipping from a robust glass of wine.

Her heart sank. Now, this was something she'd have to investigate. It was her understanding that Gink did not drink at all. Period. She thought about running into the house and demanding an explanation from her, but after mulling things over for a moment, she decided that it would be better if she spoke to her another time, after she had a chance to digest this new development.

As she sank into her car seat, she felt unease and worry in the pit of her stomach.

Chapter Eleven

Grace was feeding Clambake his dinner, when Guy Sutter, her former co-worker at San Francisco probation called. She hadn't heard from him since he had unwittingly given her significant information regarding the murder of a local resident.

"My friend won't be any trouble," Guy told her. "He's... well, he's nice. And it's only for a short time. You owe me," he reminded her.

"This is a busy time for me," Grace told him. "I'm moving my shop this week. It's so hectic. Couldn't he come another time?

"He's signed up for a writer's conference so he doesn't have any flexibility. And he doesn't have any money. You owe me, Grace."

"I got that the first time," Grace sighed. "I guess I could put him up for a few days. What's his name?"

"Felix Vanpool. You'll really like him. He won't be any trouble."

"Felix Vanpool? Is that his real name?"

"Far as I know."

"When does he want to come?"

"Tomorrow."

After putting down her phone, Grace went to the sink, filled her kettle and turned a burner on high. A cup of tea after the spaghetti dinner would surely make her feel better, she thought. She reached into her cupboard for her favorite bone china Beleek teacup, and promptly dropped it on the floor where it shattered into about a million pieces. Whereupon, she allowed herself to let out a few choice words that would shock anyone who knew her, causing Clambake to abandon his dinner and take refuge under the kitchen table.

As she dumped the last pieces of her cup into the trash, Grace decided that bed was the best option for her, and was starting up her stairs, when her phone rang again. She crossed her fingers in the hope that it would be Guy Sutter, calling her to tell her that Felix Vanpool had found a nice guesthouse in Hyannis.

However, instead of Guy, it was Andre. "Hey," he said.

"Hey, yourself," she answered recognizing Andre's voice, but surprised that he was on the other end of the line.

After a pause, Andre said, "I thought I'd call you and see how you are."

"I'm fine. Where are you?"

"I'm in my hotel. In Boston."

"Sorry, I forgot. It's been a busy day."

"Here, too. I taught a couple of death investigation classes, had dinner and watched some boring reruns and thought about you."

"Boring reruns made you think of me?"

"No, of course not," Andre laughed. "So, is everything okay?'

"Sure. Normal routine stuff. In the last couple of days, I discovered a dead body, saw one of my ospreys hanging upside down from her nest, was almost run over on Main Street, broke my favorite Irish tea cup and discovered that Gink, who, if you recall, is taking care of my dad, is drinking." She wanted to add *"..and found a note under my coffee mug that made my heart flip and sink at the same time.* But she didn't.

"Drinking? I thought she quit."

"So did I."

"Sorry to hear that." There was a long pause. The kind of pause that she knew meant that Andre was mulling things over. When the pause extended to the uncomfortable stage, she spoke again.

"And, I have a houseguest arriving tomorrow."

"One of your friends from the west coast?"

"He's a friend of Guy Sutter. Remember, the probation officer from San Francisco who helped me out last year. A friend of his needed a place to stay. He's a writer and he ..."

"He?" Andre exclaimed in a way which indicated that he was not pleased. "Why can't he get a hotel room or stay in a B&B? Cape Cod is full of places to stay."

"He doesn't have much money. Like I said, he's a writer. He's here for a conference. I couldn't say no to Guy."

"You could have."

"Guy's a friend, and I owe him."

"So, where is the houseguest staying?"

"In my spare bedroom. Where else?'

"

"That's right across the hall from yours." He made it sound like an accusation. "He could be Jack the Ripper for all you know. You should be more careful."

"Guy said he's in his late 30's, works out a lot and is nice as can be."

Grace heard him sigh. She'd made up the last part about Felix when she realized Andre was beginning to sound more than a little jealous. She had to admit, she was having fun turning the tables on him for a change.

Chapter Twelve

The beach was quiet, and the waves were lapping lightly at the shore. Two tots, running, scattering pails and shovels, were being pursued by a young mother, to the water's edge. Plovers popped out from the dunes for a look at the sea and sandpipers danced along the water's edge. Across the harbor from where Grace sat in the sand, still cool from the night air, a pale yellow glow was embracing the eastern sides of the charming wood houses that nestled close to Sandy Neck Lighthouse. She took a deep breath of the warm, early morning air. It was paradise here, she thought. Grace had grown up on the Cape, but spent several years in San Francisco, working as a probation officer. Having returned home, after her mother became ill, and her father needed her help, she stayed on, started working for Barnstable Probation, married, and was happily settled in Barnstable. Of course, much had happened in the last few years and now she was alone, a young widow with a lamp shop. But, on mornings like this one, gazing out at the sand dunes, the sea gulls bobbing in the cobalt water, a few puffy clouds floating in the pale sky, she had no doubt that she made the right decision to return home.

She had enjoyed her career as a probation officer, both in San Francisco and Barnstable. But, after Jack died, she no longer wanted to work in the courthouse, where they'd met, and where she was constantly reminded of him. Buying the lamp shop was a leap into the unknown, but she loved it, and was finally beginning to make a small income. Life was definitely good. Except, she had to admit, for Andre Cruz and his partner Emma Rice, who, in her obsessive imaginings, and despite his late night call, were probably having a romantic week in Boston. And why did he leave her that note? What was he thinking? Their relationship was over. Grace sighed as she watched fishing boats bouncing in the waves, heading out for deeper waters.

"When I first saw you, I thought you were smiling," Audrey Lee said, peering down at Grace through a pair of sleek photo chromatic glasses with pink lenses. "Now, I think it's a scowl. Anything to do with a murder at Salty Cove?"

Audrey was Grace's closest friend and former office partner at Barnstable Probation, where she still worked, which meant that she could and did keep Grace up to date about the various schemes, disagreements and other dramas that involved the Courthouse and it's denizens. They met often in the early morning before work to run along the shore.

Grace squinted up at her friend, "I'm okay. Simply indulging in some daydreaming. I'll fill you in as we run. Barefoot today?"

"Not me. I don't feel like taking off my shoes," Audrey said. "They're new, and I need to break them in."

"How did you know about the murder at Salty Cove?"

"I was Ben's probation officer," Audrey said.

"Bella and I and her hiking group discovered his body."

"Are you serious?"

"Afraid I am," Grace said. "It was awful."

"That's sad. He seemed to be finally getting his act together."

"What was his story?"

"Alcohol, hot temper and little in the way of internal control. He was difficult to supervise because he blew off his AA sessions. But, in the last few weeks, since his mother passed away, he seemed to have some focus. He told me that he was going to start a business. And, that he was in love and ready to settle down. He also mentioned that it was time to grow up. He had some new responsibilities. And since he went to two AA meetings last week I felt he was sincere."

"I saw him at Pearl's on the day he was killed," Grace told her. "I think he'd been drinking."

Audrey sighed. "So much for getting his act together."

Grace sympathized with Audrey. She knew how it felt when a probationer, after appearing to be getting his life together, took several steps backwards. She always reminded herself not to take things personally, but there were times when she couldn't help being disappointed and frustrated. That seemed to be the nature of probation work.

"Do you know his brother, William?" Grace asked.

"Yes. He came to my office once with Ben. William always went to court with him whenever there was a hearing of some kind. He seemed to want to provide Ben with support, but I'm not sure Ben welcomed his help. I sensed friction between them."

After a half hour of running, Audrey said, "You sure have a knack of discovering bodies."

"Yes, it seems that I do," Grace admitted wryly. "If the lamp shop fails, maybe I could start a career as a clairvoyant."

Audrey laughed. "I hear there's money in it."

"Well, that would be nice, too."

"Is Andre Cruz assigned to the case?" Audrey slowed to a brisk walk and placed her sunglasses up on her hair, her almond eyes peering at Grace. "Have you seen him?"

"Yes, He came by the shop last night to ask me some questions."

"What was that like?"

"Awkward. But not as awkward as when he and his partner Emma showed up at my house yesterday morning." Grace bit her lip, deciding whether or not to be completely frank. "He left me a note. He said he missed me."

"OMG! What a romantic gesture." Audrey grabbed Grace's arm. "What are you going to do?"

"I don't know. Maybe nothing. You see, I'm not sure it is a romantic gesture. I'm not sure what it meant. Come on, let's run to the parking lot."

"Maybe you should call him," Audrey suggested. "You two had something really good for a while. Maybe it's all about timing. Maybe he's ready and maybe you're ready, too?"

"That's too many maybes for me. And, I hate to admit it,

but I'm still jealous of Emma. She had a big smile when she and Andre left my house to go to Boston."

"I bet she wouldn't have been smiling if she knew about Andre's note." Audrey's breathing was steady despite the difficulty of running on the sand.

"I'm forty years old, and Emma is what? Twenty something?" Grace said, still breathing hard. Audrey, a natural athlete always kept up a fast pace, and today was no exception.

"Sure, Emma is good looking and all, but you're not exactly shabby yourself. You need more confidence."

"Thanks for the pep talk," Grace said.

"I've got to get home, change, and get to work," Audrey said, as they approached the harbor. "I've got a full schedule today."

"Me, too," Grace said, and proceeded to explain about her houseguest. "I couldn't say 'no' to Guy. He reminded me that I owe him for his help last year. He said his friend is nice and won't be in the way at all. It's such poor timing what with the chaos in my shop."

"Maybe your houseguest would be willing to lend a hand when he's not at the writer's convention."

"I hadn't thought of that. Let's hope he's strong, handsome, and willing."

"If that's the case, keep me in mind," Audrey said.

"What about Kevin?" Grace asked. "Audrey had been seeing the attractive attorney for the last few months. "I thought things were going well."

"Not really. He's not right for me. He only cares about his job."

Grace was well aware that Audrey had many interests. She was curious about the most eclectic subjects, like mushroom hunting, chess, and astrology. In the past year, she spent a lot of her free time on her family tree, tracing her family's origins to China.

"I'll keep you in mind," Grace assured her.

Walking by the harbor on the way to her cottage she was accompanied by the familiar sound of flapping sails, clacking lines, and groaning ropes. She winced, as sand that had leaked into her running shoes, now mixed with water to form a sticky abrasive. Circling around her house to the back, where she had an outside shower, Grace started worrying about all the things she had to do. Her house would need to be picked up and vacuumed. The kitchen should be cleaned up, too. She'd put things off, because of the extra work at the shop. Now, with a houseguest arriving, even a flat broke writer she didn't know, she felt compelled to get everything in order. And what about food? Did she need to shop for him as well? Grace laughed to herself when she realized that she was obsessing over something other than Emma Rice. Which was a good thing, because a clean house was something she could take care of.

Chapter Thirteen

Grace stepped into the wood enclosure that sheltered her outdoor shower. Bathing outside was something she had never done in Northern California. Here, she could look up at the trees and sky, could see the clouds float by, and glimpse sea gulls and ospreys as they flew overhead, or watch, as she was doing now, a bluish green hummingbird hovering around the morning glory blossoms that crept along the edge of the shower. Soaping up her hair with lavender shampoo, she was humming the second verse of a light jazzy tune she'd been unable to get out of her head, when she heard a swishing noise in her uncut grass. Leaning away from the splashing shower, she tried to detect the direction the sound was coming from and decided that it was the wind sweeping in from the marsh.

She was continuing to massage her scalp when she heard the same swishing noise again, only this time it was decidedly closer. Perhaps Trixie, her neighbor's Maltese, had escaped her yard and slithered under the salt spray roses, despite the tiny thorns.

Shutting off the water, she reached for her towel on top of the stall, where she'd flung it in her haste, only to have it slip through her fingers and fall to the ground outside of the enclosure. The sound of breathing, now very close, made her sure that something much larger than Trixie was approaching.

"Who's there?" she called out.

But her question was met with silence as water ran down her sides and shampoo dripped into her eyes.

Deciding to risk opening the door, she was pulling on the latch, when she heard a rustle in the morning glories. A large hand appeared on the edge of the shower. Screaming, she armed herself with her back scrubbing brush.

A head full of frizzy brown hair popped up above the rim and she brought her brush down hard. She was about to give it another good whack when she heard a male voice. "Ouch! Oh gosh. Grace Tolliver?"

"Who the hell are you?" Grace asked, her temper catching up to her embarrassment.

"I'm Felix!" the man said. "I caught an early bus. Here's your towel. Don't worry I didn't see anything. This is very cool. I love outdoor showers. Can't wait to try it out."

Her houseguest, it seemed had arrived.

Chapter Fourteen

Grace's classic Cape Cod cottage, covered with weathered gray shingles was more than one hundred and fifty years old. This past spring she'd finally found a free weekend to scrape and paint her front shutters a creamy oyster shell. Her front garden was half lawn, half flowers, with a large cherry tree and two smaller pears. The hydrangeas under her bay window, a beautiful pink in spring, were now spent, as were a cluster of white cleomes. The grass needed mowing, and her bird feeders needed seed. The garden and house were a never- ending chore, but she felt safe and comforted when she gazed out of her window, through the wavy glass of the original panes, at her mostly dead, but beloved yard.

The back of her house faced what she possessively referred to as 'her marsh', a small piece of the more than 3,000 acres of salt marsh that bordered the village. From her rear windows, she could see Sandy Neck, a spit of land that extended into Cape Cod Bay. It would be nice to see the lighthouse, but she wasn't complaining. Her view of marsh, water, and sand dunes was thrilling enough.

Now, Grace was sitting in her den that she had converted into a workroom. It was convenient to work at home, often late at night, a cup of tea, or on some occasions, a glass of chardonnay at her side. There was a large pine table in the middle of the room, and boxes of lamps were stacked on every available surface, to be returned to the shop when the construction work was done.

Earlier, Grace had called Michael. She told him that she would work at home today. He said he'd be at the shop, finishing up some painting projects, but would leave around noon.

"Everything is good, here," Michael said. "The crew worked late last night, and the old wood floors look very nice. Not exactly what I know you wanted, but most of the marks and dents from Beaus' bookshelves have been smoothed out."

"Good news," Grace said. "I think we can open the day after tomorrow. Everything won't be perfect, but then it never is. At last we'll be getting back to normal."

"Normal around here is a relative thing. Especially with Duane around," Michael said. "He spent most of the day looking for a couple of lamps he'd tucked away somewhere. I don't think he found them, because he said something about his system breaking down. But, with Beau's help, he hauled in that lovely Persian carpet that belonged to your grandmother."

Grace remembered what a good sport Beau had been about letting her keep some items upstairs until the work was done. And when she brought in her carpet, and the floor wasn't done, he'd stored it in his loft, out of harm's way.

Beau told her he was a former college librarian from Vermont. After going through a painful and difficult divorce, he decided to relocate and pursue a dream of owning a bookstore. Starting over, ups and downs notwithstanding, he was steadily re building his life. Grace thought that he was a good influence on Duane, as well. Certainly he was able to relate to him in a way that the others had not.

Duane had grown up in foster homes without much in the way of positive role models. Now, on his own, with a job, he was doing well, but was still very immature, most likely a result of his years abusing drugs.

"What shade are you working on?" Michael asked her now.

"It's really two matching shades for a toddler's bedroom," Grace said. "I've finished the background, a soft purpley color. As soon as they're ready, I'm going to paint circus figures in deep violet, dancing in silhouette around the bottom. I'll put a hint of a circus tent edge along the top."

"I don't think purpley is a word, but I'm sure it's very nice," Michael said. "Your paintings are lovely although your early efforts were rather, how shall I put it?... oops, here's Bella."

Grace could hear Bella whispering sharply to Michael. She could envision her shaking a warning fist at him.

"Grace, I'm going to go home, have a nap, and change into something suitable for my godson's wake," Bella said, clearly having wrested the phone from Michael. "I'll be ready when you come to get me. I do appreciate the ride. I'm not sure I'm up to going alone, don't you know?"

She did. She was more than happy to take Bella, particularly since she wasn't keen on going alone herself. After all, she hadn't known Ben. But, she feared she would never forget his cold blue eyes as she lifted his head out of the water.

She smoothed her hands over a piece of crisp, white linen. Judging from what customers told her they were surprised to see that a shade wasn't painted while it hung on the lamp. Now, she gently touched her watercolor to see if it was dry enough to start on the silhouettes when she heard the front door slam, shaking the old glass in the windows. Could it be Felix, back so soon from a walk to the village? She looked up from her work.

"I've brought you a hostess gift," Felix said, smiling from ear to ear, as he gingerly held out a three-foot cactus, with dozens of six-inch long spikes. "Guy told me you liked flowers."

Chapter Fifteen

The funeral home, a lovely lavender clapboard was welcoming, despite the dreary circumstances. The house was brilliantly lit up, the pathways, the porch, and the entryway beckoning toward the deceased. It was an hour before sunset, and the evening was still so hot, that Bella brought out a folded fan from her purse. Soon, light breezes from Cape Cod Bay would chase away the mosquitoes, after their last taste of blood. White chrysanthemums crowded out some purple cornflowers for space in pots, and planter boxes spread out on the porch and under the front windows. Grace could see numerous people milling about on the stairs and through the open doorway.

"Quite a few folks here tonight," Grace said to Bella.

"Ben lived here all of his life, and Imogene had so many friends."

Grace felt pressure on her elbow and turned around. "Dad! What are you doing here?"

Thomas De Pace gave Grace a little kiss on her cheek as he reached out for Bella's hand. "Evening, Bella. Sorry about Ben."

"Thank you, Thomas. Poor Ben. Such a frightful thing to happen to him."

"You're right there," he said. "I'm mainly here out of respect for Imogene. I knew her just about all of my life. I'm glad that she isn't around to see this."

"Where's Gink?" Grace asked.

"She dropped me off. Muttered something about being 'creeped out by dead people,' and said she'd be back to get me in half an hour."

That's odd, Grace thought. After all, Gink had known Ben

and his family for many years. She knew she needed to talk to her dad about Gink, and soon, but she also knew he might raise a ruckus when she did, and that was exactly what she didn't need right now.

Grace followed Bella and her father into the wake, uncomfortably aware that not a few people were watching them. She supposed they were thinking of their discovery of Ben's body, and their jumping in his pool, trying to save him. Perhaps they even considered them suspects; after all, they had been the first on the scene. Oh well, nothing she could do about the thoughts of others. She'd best wander around and talk to some people, have a cookie or two and perhaps even learn more about Ben.

Drifting through crowded rooms, Grace observed an interesting mix of folks. Several men and women, who were probably Imogene's friends, were perched on chairs and sofas in the front room, sharing stories as if they were at a high school reunion. She watched as Bella and her father were welcomed into the group.

Other cheerless souls, with rough skin, now and then missing a tooth or two, roamed around the visiting rooms. Grace spotted a couple of them passing around a bottle of spirits, perhaps Ben's favorite. There was even some laughter that floated above the murmurs and tears. Grace recognized a few people, some from the lamp shop, some from the courthouse, and some she figured she had seen here and there around the Cape, which after all, wasn't a very big community. Wandering over to the room where Ben's body had been laid out in a simple casket, she recognized Ben's neighbor, Roone Seymoor, looking elegant in a dark suit, his thick auburn hair appearing to be purposely tousled. He was speaking urgently to a blonde woman she had never seen before.

"When poor Imogene died, I offered Ben a fair price, but he wouldn't budge," Roone said, loud enough for Grace to hear. "He talked about a B&B. Can you imagine? Between you and me, I wish the whole house would burn down. It's such an eyesore and it obstructs my view of the water. When Imogene let the landscapers go, it was the final straw. Every time I look out my window, what do I see? A disaster, that's what!"

The woman, her blond hair in a neat chignon and dressed in black, except for a brilliant emerald green scarf, placed a hand on his sleeve. "I couldn't agree more, Roone," she said softly.

"But, now that Ben is gone, I feel like the place is in hand." Roone made a fist. "Luna, trust me, none of us neighbors will have to worry about any ridiculous inn or guest house in that run down place. William has indicated to me that he and Portia will want to sell the property as soon as possible."

"That's such a relief," she assured him. "I know you'll take care of it. Keeping up property values is so important to us all."

"It will be cared for, or it will disappear, I promise you, dear Luna," Roone replied, clearly unaware of Grace's presence, he leaned over and kissed his companion quickly but passionately on her neck, right below a flirtatiously dangling earring of cascading pearls. Pursing her lips in response, Luna smiled up at him and drifted away.

So, Grace thought, Ben wasn't even buried yet, and some neighbors are making plans to take over his property.

Deciding she needed some coffee and some food, which was being served in the next room, she spotted Officer Gelb sitting by himself. A nice table lamp made from a cut glass vase, inches from his elbow, cast a dim glow on his gold watchband. She almost didn't recognize him, not because of the potted palm and shadows that shielded him, but because of his changed appearance from the Officer Gelb she'd met when he responded to a burglary at her house last winter. Then, with his fuzzy, pale hair and skinny physique, he'd looked too young to be out alone by himself at night. Now, he appeared more mature, and she noted his muscled physique as he ran a hand over his shiny, bald scalp. He managed to surprise her after all.

She started to walk over to him, say hello, and see if she could find out some details or gossip about the murder. After all, she had been the one who called 911. But as she approached, he said, "Can't talk. On duty."

"Oh, right," Grace said, thinking that, despite his tough

appearance, the young officer was insecure. Turning away, she saw Audrey standing behind a table fiddling with the lid of a coffee pot. Maybe there would be some cookies over there.

"Hi Grace," Audrey said pouring a dark liquid into a cup. "Want some coffee?"

"Decaf, please. I didn't know you were coming tonight."

"I try to go to the funerals of my probationers. You know, show respect. Luckily, for me, there have only been a few." She nodded toward the door. "I saw your dad and Bella in the other room. Your father looks good, but Bella looks tired."

"It's been a difficult couple of days. Finding Ben in his pool was such a shock."

"No kidding," Audrey said. "And what about you? You're going to get a reputation, showing up at murder scenes the way you do."

Grace made no reply, but she did wonder how many other people were thinking the same thing.

A petite woman with fine hair, the color of a robin's breast, which swirled imaginatively around her small head, and wearing dangerously high heels, pushed her way roughly between Audrey and Grace. She held her arm high in the air, as if to be sure that everyone could see the large diamond bracelet that sparkled on her tiny wrist.

"Where's Ben's body? I want to see him," she sobbed. "He was my fiancée. I can't believe this. Who are all of these people?" she added, to no one in particular, as she pushed her small frame through the crowd, eliciting stares and looks of anger from the mourners.

A slim woman with dark hair blocked her way into the viewing area. The hysterical woman backed away from her and straggled off in the direction of the crowd with the bottle of spirits.

"She's a real piece of work, that one," William said, as he appeared at Grace's side.

"That's Freesia Foster," Grace told him. "I was her probation officer a few years ago. She acted like she didn't recognize me, but I'm quite certain she did. Although probationers may want to forget their P.O.'s in my experience, few do."

Audrey nodded.

"Nice to see you, Ms. Lee," William said to Audrey. "Thank you for your help with Ben."

"I was sorry to hear about his death," Audrey replied. "Lately, he seemed to be more motivated to turn things around, attending his court-ordered alcohol counseling. It must be difficult for you. I know you did a lot for him."

"Yes, thank you. Very difficult," William agreed. "Not that Ben was a prince, but he was my brother. This is my wife, Morgan," he added, introducing a woman dressed in a cream silk suit, who had appeared at his side.

"So sad. Thank you both for coming," Morgan began, only to be interrupted by an ear splitting yowl emitting from the viewing room.

William looked at the floor, and closed his eyes for a second or two. "Darn! I've got to escort that woman out of here. Fiancé? Ben didn't tell me anything about getting married. What is she talking about? She turned Ben down when he proposed to her last year, and took up with his best friend, Mason Crawford. Now, she's drunk or high or something, and it's up to me to take her outside."

"Need help?" Audrey asked.

"Nah. If I do, I can always call on Mr. Muscle, over there, under the palm."

"She's not driving I hope?"

"No. Mason dropped her off. At least he had the decency to stay away tonight." As a high pitched wailing pierced the air, William grimaced, and left them standing amidst the crowd, holding their empty coffee cups, and at least, on Grace's part, wondering if decency was the reason that Mason hadn't come to his best friend's wake.

*****

Since Bella was taking her time with her goodbyes, Grace waited for her outside on the porch where she found a comfy, unoccupied swing chaise, covered in cheery purple and red chintz. She had settled into it, when she was drawn to a noise at the window. Peering through the gauzy curtains, she was surprised to see Roone still in the viewing room, apparently in deep thought, and drumming his fingers on the edge of Ben's casket. His demeanor changed as someone out of Grace's range of vision entered the room.

"Portia, I'm so sorry," he said. "What a difficult time for you and William. And so soon after Imogene's death."

"Thank you, Roone."

Grace strained to see Portia, but as a group of mourners mounted the porch steps, she hastily turned away from the window. When she was alone again, she leaned forward pushing chrysanthemums out of her way to get a better view into the room. Portia, a tall, very thin woman, dressed in a black lace cocktail dress and glittery gold sandals, was now standing with her back to the window, leaning over the casket. Roone moved to her side and spoke in a hushed tone that Grace strained to hear.

"Not now Roone," she said in a clear voice when he was finished. "This is not the time or place. I'm well aware what you want. We'll talk another time."

Roone, looking exasperated, turned as a dark haired, attractive woman, with thick bangs and shoulder length hair, who Grace recognized as the one who had blocked Freesia's entry into the room, moved at a snail's pace toward the casket, dabbing at her eyes with a tissue.

"Ah, here's my lovely wife. Julia," Roone said. "Darling, are you ready to go?"

Grace's mouth dropped. Wife? This woman? What about the silky blonde with the dangling earrings that he had been kissing just a short time ago? Roone held out his hand, but Julia ignored it, and giving him a withering glance, turned to Portia. "We'll see you at church tomorrow morning," she said. "I didn't see Trevor here tonight, but please give him my sympathies."

"Thank you Julia. My husband is not feeling well." Portia said. "He wanted to rest up, so that he would be at his best. We have a busy week ahead of us."

Julia and Roone exchanged a few more words of condolence, and then left the room together, but Grace could see by her body language that Julia was upset about something. She didn't know the woman, but there was something sullen and unforgiving in the look that she gave her husband, which might well indicate that she had witnessed him and the attractive Luna, flirting over Ben's dead body.

Portia, leaned over the casket again and muttered a few indistinguishable words to her deceased brother, and then walked over to the window and stood behind the curtain, through which Grace could see the face of the silver haired driver of the Mercedes that had almost run into her on Main St. She tried to recollect the argument that spilled out of the Mercedes as it almost collided with her. Someone had a problem and something was missing, but, what it was all about made no sense to her.

*****

Grace kissed her dad goodnight as he settled himself in his car, before walking around to Gink, sitting behind the wheel, and leaning over her.

"I saw you drinking wine the other night," Grace said in a low voice. "Any more of that and you're out on the street. You know where to get help. Understood?"

Gink looked surprised, but quickly recovered. "I understand. It won't happen again."

"What's that?" her father asked.

"Nothing Dad," Grace assured him.

"Did you know that Thomas is adding a small addition to the back of the house?" Gink asked, apparently not overly concerned that she had been caught out.

"Dad, what are you thinking?" Grace exclaimed. "You've got a big house. Why do you need an addition?"

"I thought I might move my photography studio from the shed out back," her father replied. "You know it needs a new roof."

As a professional photographer, he occasionally took on a

small job, although he was now for the most part, retired. He had quite a lot of equipment in his shed, and he was right, it did need a new roof.

"You've got four bedrooms, an attic, a basement and a garage," Grace protested. "I'll help you move your stuff to any one of those places. You don't need an addition."

"Gives me something to do, Gracie. I'm bored."

"Oh Lord," said Grace. "Gink, is it too late to stop this project?"

"Not sure, but I'm trying." Gink told her. "He was up at five o' clock this morning laying out tools to knock a hole in the wall. But, so far everything's still intact."

Grace's father chuckled again. "I like to get up early," he declared as though articulating a special virtue.

"You like to get up early so no one can see what you're up to," Grace scolded.

Thomas winked at her. Grace was relieved to see that Gink appeared to be sober, however, she hadn't imagined that big glass of wine she'd seen the young woman drinking from, just last night. At least she'd given her warning, and she had no doubt that Gink knew she meant business.

Gink and her dad both waved as they pulled away. Grace loved her father dearly, but he could be a handful. It was a challenge, to keep him safe but not dampen his spirit. Her mother had faced this issue for decades but she had had a way of keeping him on course, and since her mother's death, her father had no one but Grace to put on the brakes. She recognized that many of his 'projects' were designed to get her attention, and as a consequence, was getting better at seeing the humor in her dad's schemes and manipulations. At least she hoped she was.

*****

"Turn left here," Bella said when they approached Pine Street, as if Grace hadn't been to Bella's house a dozen times before tonight. "Portia told me that she wants me to meet her at Salty Cove as soon as possible. Next driveway Grace," she directed. "She wants my opinion on some antique lamps that were Imogene's. I asked her to bring William and Trevor. I do need to talk to them all about some family things."

Grace's cell rang. "Don't go answering that while you're driving," Bella said. "It's against the law."

"I know," Grace said, coasting to a stop by Bella's mailbox, wishing she could answer the call. If Bella hadn't been there, she might have.

"By the way, did you see that woman who said she was Ben's fiancée?" Bella asked.

"Yes, Freesia Foster. I know her. She did seem very distraught."

"Ben told me that he and Freesia were back together, this time for keeps and were planning to marry. Ben had a good many girlfriends, but I do believe he was quite serious about Freesia. They were going to run the B&B together. I know he seemed disagreeable to you, Grace, but he was doing better than he had in a long time. Things were looking up for him."

"He wasn't sober when I met him," Grace said.

"I know, but I do think he was trying to quit. Not succeeding but trying harder." Bella sounded a bit defensive, Grace thought.

"I'm wondering if he was beginning to feel more secure with Freesia," Bella said. "I noticed that she was wearing a bracelet that I'm pretty darn sure belonged to Imogene."

"It was hard to miss all of those sparkly diamonds." Grace agreed, deciding that this was not the time to tell Bella about Freesia's criminal record. "Do you think it odd that Imogene left the house to Ben?" Grace asked.

"I know she would have treated all of her children fairly. I'm sure that William and Portia's investments would have more than compensated for the property she left Ben. She couldn't have foreseen the economic downturn, but I have no doubt about her intentions. She knew that they would probably want to sell the old place, and Ben couldn't possibly buy them out. I understand what she wanted to do," Bella sighed. "But, I've come to learn that things don't always go as planned."

"That's for sure," Grace agreed. "Guess I better make a

will. Now that I have the shop and all."

"And Clambake," Bella said.

"Of course," Grace shut off the ignition and rolled down her window, the cool interior air mingling with the warm night breeze.

"I know Imogene wanted Ben to have something of his own," Bella said, fumbling in her purse for her house keys. "She encouraged him in his B&B idea, although I doubt the neighbors out there would be too keen on that. Everything has changed now, hasn't it?"

"If Salty Cove is sold, it may end up in the hands of someone who wants to tear it down," Grace said, remembering Roone and Luna discussing the property.

"It would be such a shame if someone tore it down and built one of those big up-to-the-minute things."

"That's a depressing thought." Grace said, imagining a monster of a house replacing the stately old home. "Did you see William, Ben, and Portia often?"

"Not really. William drops by the shop sometimes during a break from court to say hello, I've been to Portia's house many times throughout the years, but not lately. I saw Ben more often. When I went over to see Imogene, the three of us would visit and have ourselves a cigar."

"What's with the cigars?" Grace asked, "I was surprised to hear that you were smoking one the other day."

Bella chortled. "The Walwyn's made a good share of their money by importing cigars. So, they all enjoyed, and, dare I say, encouraged cigar smoking. It was a family thing, and since I was like a family member, being Ben's godmother and all, I started joining them. Only very occasionally, of course."

"A nice memory."

"Yes," Bella repeated, her eyes watering. "Ben ran with a rough crowd, but who would want to kill him? I feel that I owe it to Imogene to find out who murdered her son. And, doesn't that fall into godmother duties?"

Bella turned away from Grace, swung her sturdy bottom sideways and with a grumble planted her feet on the driveway. "I want you to help me find out who killed Ben," she said, over her shoulder, slamming the door shut before Grace could utter a word.

Chapter Sixteen

Clambake paced the kitchen floor, jumped on the counter, and was quickly ejected by Grace.

"Come on, Clambake," she said, carefully measuring cat food into a bowl. I'm only a little late, and you know you're not allowed on the counter." She carefully measured cat food into a bowl. "You've got to lose some weight, you know. The vet said that you're a twelve pound cat that weighs seventeen."

Felix was sitting at the table, a super-sized cola in his hand. "I would have fed the cat," he said, "but I wasn't sure what to do. He sat on my lap today when I was on the patio."

When Grace put the food on the floor, Clambake pounced on it. It was true, she had been so busy the past week that she hadn't been able to give her oversized cat the attention he deserved, and he was definitely in need of a good brushing. She'd be sure to snuggle up with him tonight. But, right now, she had to set Felix straight on her most important house rule. "I told you, Clambake is not supposed to go outside. He's an inside only cat. And if I get delayed again, the cat food is in the pantry."

"Oh, sorry. He wanted to go out with me, so I thought it would be okay. I like him. We're a couple of big guys."

Yes, indeed, Grace thought. Felix was at least six foot three and broad shouldered. If he didn't have that wild frizzy hair and if he had a better personality, he might even be attractive. That thought was so disturbing to Grace that she immediately put it out of her mind. She went back to viewing him as totally repulsive. But, he looked plenty strong enough to help her move a few boxes of lamps back to the shop.

Grace placed the last of a selection of soda glasses, plates, and silverware in the dishwasher. Felix was not going to be easy. When she had come home last night, after visiting her father and Gink, she found the front door unlocked, sand tracked on her beautiful pumpkin pine floors and a half full carton of milk turning sour on the kitchen counter. Of course, she'd spoken to him about it. He was most apologetic and promised to clean up his act. And, that ridiculous cactus he gave her looked like something that belonged in a horror movie. As soon as she could, she'd put it in her barn where it might scare off unwelcome creatures.

"How's the writing conference?" she asked.

"Good. Real good. I'm learning a lot."

"What kind of writing do you do?"

"I'm all about journalism. That's why I always have my notebook with me." Felix patted his breast pocket.

"Uh, Felix, you have anything going on tonight? Because, if you don't, I'd appreciate it if you would help me move some boxes of lamps back to my shop. I've had to store them here during the remodel, and now it's time to get them back. It will take a half hour or so."

"Yeah, sure," Felix's said without enthusiasm. "You want to do it now?"

"Yes, it's getting late and I'm tired. Let's load up my car and be done with it."

She was looking forward to a serious talk with Guy Sutter. After a week with Felix, she wouldn't owe him anything, that's for sure.

*****

Grace perched a carton on her bent knee as she unlocked the door to Pearl's and propped open the door for Felix, who was easily handling a heavy box.

"Hey, this is kind of interesting," Felix said, glancing around the shop. "I have an assignment to write about something or someplace unusual. You know a curious, odd kind of place. Mind if I poke around and see what kind of stuff you've got in here?"

"Okay, but be quick. I don't want to linger." Grace said,

although she hadn't thought of Pearl's as odd and curious. Instead, she preferred, charming, beautiful, and full of creative energy.

"Where do you want me to put these boxes?"

"Take them to the first room down the hall on the right," Grace said, watching Felix weave slowly across the room, his head swiveling side to side, seeming to take in as much of Pearl's as he possibly could. What was he up to? She wondered. He couldn't really be planning on writing about her antique lamp shop.

"What the ...?" Grace heard Felix yell, followed by the slamming of the back door. Hearing a motor starting up, Grace ran back down the front porch steps and around the corner of the building, and saw a light colored vehicle traveling down the side driveway with Felix in pursuit. Standing in front of it, she shouted, "Hey! Stop!"

To her astonishment the vehicle leaped forward, moving toward her at a surprising rate of speed. Surely the driver would stop. But they didn't.

Flung across the hood, she seized one of the windshield wipers and held on as the driver bumped over the curb and headed east on Main Street. "Grace!" She heard Felix yell, "Let go!"

Grace landed none too gently, in a flowerbed that bordered one of the stately homes on the street. She lay there for a minute, collecting herself and staring up at the limbs of an ancient oak tree. Part of a broken windshield wiper was clutched in her hand.

"Are you all right?" Felix said, crouching down beside her.

"I think so." Grace sat up brushing black-eyed Susans out of her eyes and hair, and feeling a burn in her right knee and shoulder. "Seriously, I'm okay," she said, letting him pull her to her feet.

Felix held onto her arm. "Are you insane? What do you think you were doing, hanging onto the wipers? You could have been killed."

"I heard you yell, went out and tried to stop the car. Before I knew it, it was coming at me, and I was hanging on for dear life. Did you see the driver?"

Felix shook his head from side to side. "Unfortunately, no. We better call the police. Are you sure you're all right?" he added as she rubbed the back of her head. "Maybe you need an ambulance."

"No, no ambulance! But, let's call the police and report a prowler at my shop."

Felix was already dialing 911 on his cell. He spoke swiftly to the dispatcher and hung up. It was, she realized, odd how Felix seemed to be taking charge of the situation in a way that she couldn't have imagined an hour ago. Maybe she bumped her head harder than she first thought. Hopefully, it was not a concussion. The idea that Felix could be anything but useless was certainly a surprise.

*****

Grace and Felix talked to the police, and after the report was made, Felix drove them home. Neither of them had much in the way of useful information to pass on to the officers, since everything had happened so fast. Felix had heard someone rattle the handle on the back door and gone charging after them. Although, he hadn't caught the license plate number, they both agreed it was an older model sedan, possibly gray with a Red Socks bumper sticker, not unlike half the cars on the Cape. Neither of them was certain if the driver was a male or a female.

"Thanks, Felix. I appreciate your help," Grace said, never having imagined that she'd need to thank him for anything other than possibly leaving her house earlier than planned.

A car door slammed, startling Grace. Pulling back her curtain, she saw Andre getting out of his car.

Felix said as long as Grace was okay, and had company, he was going to walk around a bit. He'd be back later. He went out the back door as she greeted André at the front steps. It was almost like one of those silly old movies where the lover slid out the back as the husband slipped in the front.

*****

"You okay?" Andre asked managing to look concerned and amused at the same time. Of course, the whole episode was embarrassing. Flinging herself on the hood of a car and ending up with her face planted in a flowerbed. Still, Grace decided not to mention her concern about a possible concussion. If she did, Andre would interrogate her about why she thought she might have a concussion in the first place, and then she would start telling him about Felix. Instead, she asked, "How did you find out so fast?"

Ignoring the question, Andre removed a flower and some leaves from her hair and then poured her a drink of scotch, which she didn't think she needed, didn't particularly care for, and only had around the house for company. She managed to take a sip.

"Good. Now take another," he told her. "I know you're tired, but I want to talk about some of these things that are happening. You up for a couple of questions?"

"Of course," she said, even though all she wanted was a shower and her bed.

"Okay. Give me that windshield wiper you're holding in your hand. Now, you were with someone tonight. Who was he?"

"A friend was helping me with some boxes. His name is Felix."

"Felix who?"

"Felix Vanpool."

"That's an odd name."

"What has this got to do with anything?" She was definitely tired now, and fear and fatigue meant a spate of crankiness was coming on.

He took a deep breath. "What's your take on what happened tonight?"

"Someone was trying to get into my shop."

"Do you think someone was after something or that someone might be looking for you?'

"Why would anyone be looking for me?"

"You found Ben's body. The Medical Examiner said he hadn't been dead for even an hour before you arrived on the scene. Whoever killed him may think that you might have seen them."

Grace could feel her heart beating. "Oh my God," she gasped. "Do you think so? Am I in any danger?"

"You could be."

Andre walked to the door and stared into her dark front lawn. After a minute, he turned away from the screen and closed the door. "I think I better stay here tonight."

"That's nice of you," Grace stammered. "But, it's not necessary. I've got good locks all around, and my houseguest will probably be here soon. I won't be alone."

"I'll sleep in my car," Andre said, with what Grace thought was irritation in his voice.

"Okay," she replied, realizing that one way or another Andre was going to stay the night. "Sleep on the couch, but don't shoot my houseguest when he comes home."

*****

When Grace woke with a start the next morning, Andre was standing over her holding a cup of coffee. Grabbing the duvet, folded at the bottom of her bed, she pulled it up to her chin.

"Don't be ridiculous." Andre grinned and handed her the cup of French Roast. "It's too hot for that blanket and it's not like I haven't seen you..."

Grace shot him a look and took a tentative sip of the hot black coffee.

"Ugh!" she muttered. "Cop coffee."

She liked hers with cream and sugar. Apparently, Andre had forgotten. Still, she supposed it was thoughtful of him to bring her a cup.

"I thought you would be gone by now," she said. "You startled me."

"I think I deserve thanks for sleeping on that tiny loveseat of yours," he said, taking the cup and helping himself to a gulp. Not that I haven't slept in worse conditions. "Clambake likes me though. He slept on my feet most of the night."

Grace looked at him skeptically. "Clambake always sleeps

with me."

"Go ahead. Ask him," Andre said playfully.

Grace, still in shock that he was in her bedroom, was not in the mood for Andre's games. "I need to get up and feed him. Why don't you go downstairs? I'll be down in a minute."

"Take your time, Grace. I've already fed him." Andre assured her finishing off the coffee.

"Wait, isn't that my coffee?"

"Nope, this is mine. There's more in the pot. You do like yours with cream and sugar, don't you?"

He smiled, a dimple piercing his left cheek. "Adeus," he said. "I've got to go. I'll check in with you later. And, by the way, there's no sign of your houseguest. Maybe he's found himself a lover. Lucky guy."

Grace leaned back on her pillows. He could be so obnoxious, she thought. But, he *had* remembered how she liked her coffee. Now, she wondered if that was a good thing or not.

Chapter Seventeen

It was six in the morning, and Clambake was fast asleep in his bed by the fireplace. There was no sign of Felix, so maybe Andre was right. It was hard to imagine, but it was possible Felix had met someone at the writers' conference. He'd certainly left in a hurry last night when Andre arrived.

Grace rubbed her head and peered at herself in the hall mirror. Although she had a headache, there was no visible injury to her face, but there was a large bruise on her elbow and a cut on her knee. Other than a general stiffness, she didn't feel too bad, considering her wild ride on the hood of some crazy person's car. What bothered her most was why anyone would break into Pearl's. She didn't keep a lot of cash around. Although some lamps had considerable value, none seemed worth burglarizing her store.

This morning, a gentle mist was hovering over the marsh, without even a breeze to rattle the tall grasses. She decided it might be a good time to take a walk and check on her ospreys, or sea hawks, as they were also known. She'd spent more time than she cared to admit peering through her binoculars at the fascinating creatures as two adults raised three chicks. When she got close to the nest, she could see that it was seriously sagging after a summer of intense use by the birds. She figured all it needed was a strong breeze, and it would be down.

It was pleasant out on the marsh in the early morning. When she was troubled, lonely, or simply wanted a breath of fresh air to clear her mind, she would step out her back door and soak up the wild, unique serenity. Of course, the Great Marsh had its moods. At any time, any season, storms might swoop down on the quiet water and whip it into a frenzy of wind and grass, sea and silt, snow and ice. She often watched, holding her breath, as nature's fury descended on her cottage.

As Grace approached her back porch she could smell coffee brewing. Opening up the screen door, she picked up Clambake as he tried to launch himself toward freedom, and placed him on a kitchen chair. She didn't want him out chasing birds, or worse, getting hurt by a raccoon or other wild animal. After all, it wasn't that long ago, a bear spent several days sniffing around the shores of Cape Cod, and the last thing she needed was a bear attack.

Almost as startling as thoughts of bears was the scene she encountered in her kitchen. Felix and Bella were sitting at her table, each with a mug of coffee, noisily munching on fresh pastry. Her houseguest, dressed in khaki shorts, sandals, and a blue tee shirt covered with crumbs was telling Bella how he had saved Grace's life the previous night.

"Morning Grace," Bella said, taking a bite of her muffin, and leaving Felix to return to his plate filled with scrambled eggs and bacon. "Apparently, someone broke into Salty Cove last night too. William called and asked me to come and take a look around with him, because I know the place so well. He's not sure what, if anything, is missing. I thought you'd want to come with me, since we're investigating the case together. You can fill me in on the way about the incident at Pearl's. We must get to the bottom of this!"

"Ah," Grace thought. Bella's not so subtle pressure was beginning. Still, she couldn't really be serious about trying to find out who murdered Ben. Finding his body had been frightening enough. Whoever killed him was a vicious killer. The whole incident was best left to the police.

But she couldn't let Bella go out there without her. What if there *was* some connection between the two incidents? And what if William *was* Ben's killer? After all, with Ben out of the way, he would now inherit half of Imogene's estate.

Getting up from the table, Felix dropped his plate, a skillet with sticky egg residue, and his cup in the sink. "I've got an early class today," he said, gathering up a stack of notebooks and pens. "Nice meeting up with you, Bella."

"Interesting houseguest," Bella said as the door shut behind him.

"Interesting isn't the word that first comes to my mind but, it will do for now," Grace called back, over her shoulder, as she ran upstairs to get ready to go to Salty Cove, returning a few minutes later carrying an umbrella and a stack of empire shades.

"Is rain predicted? Surely, this mist will blow over soon."

"I can't take any chances. These are very fragile hand cut shades. Some of them are painted in watercolor on silk paper."

"William will be waiting for us," Bella said. "It does seem like the perfect opportunity to go to Salty Cove and snoop around. And, with this latest development, maybe we can pick up some clues."

Remembering the last time she and Bella had visited Salty Cove where one of the Walwyn brothers would be waiting, Grace shuddered. With any luck, there would be no surprises today.

Chapter Eighteen

Grace closed her eyes as Bella hurtled her old Volvo down the potholed sandy driveway toward the big house where they had found Ben's body less than a week ago. Her neck was wet with sweat, although she wasn't sure whether that was because of the muggy air or the sheer terror of riding with Bella.

The mist had moved on and droplets of rain were cascading down the windshield. Bella screeched to a stop in front of the house, as William, dressed in jeans and plaid shirt, plastic gloves on both hands and arms loaded with two bulky garbage bags, emerged through the front door. Grace, who was used to seeing him a suit and tie, was surprised to discover that he appeared leaner and yet more muscular than she had realized.

"Hey, ladies," William said. "Come inside. You're going to get soaked."

They followed him into the front hallway, where Bella stopped, her hand over her chest. "Oh my," she exclaimed. "I didn't realize how difficult this would be. I spent so much time here with Imogene and Ben. And, of course, you and Portia, when you were kids."

"It was a lovely place back then. Unfortunately, Ben didn't keep up with things and the place is a mess. Portia and I are still hashing things out, but I expect we will sell. There's a neighbor just up the hill, Roone Seymoor. He told me that he'd like to make an offer. And, if that doesn't work out, there are plenty of buyers who'd love to have waterfront, despite the condition of the house."

"I know Roone," Bella said. "He stops by Pearl's every now and then for lamp repairs or a new shade. He and his wife, Julia, even had me come out to their house to appraise a lamp that they inherited. They're very sophisticated antique collectors. Especially Roone. The lamp in question was awfully nice. A Pairpoint Puffy."

"I've always wanted to see one of those," Grace said wistfully.

"Speaking of lamps," William said, maneuvering past them with another plastic garbage bag. "I've been looking around here trying to find out what might have been taken during the break-in. I'm making a list of things that I can't locate. I'm also going through all of the papers that were scattered around. I'm hoping that you may be able to help me, specifically of course, with any lamps that Mom had that might be of value. And, if you think anything is missing, let me know. "Morgan's in the kitchen making ice tea. Help yourselves to anything in the fridge," he said, as he headed toward the back door.

"Follow me, Grace," Bella said, "We'll tour the house and check out the lamps as we go. Did you bring a notebook? No? How do you expect to investigate a murder when you don't have a notebook?"

*****

An hour later, Bella and Grace were sitting on a lumpy sofa under lattice windows cranked open to let the hot, soggy breeze find its way, into the house from the nearby sea.

William and his wife, Morgan, were lounging in a pair of overstuffed striped chairs, their feet resting on matching ottomans.

"William, dear, I saw Portia and Trevor pull into the drive a few minutes ago," Morgan said. "They're still sitting in the car."

"Probably arguing," William said.

"Between you and me," Bella whispered to Grace, "I never was too fond of Portia. She's a bit bratty, if you know what I mean."

Grace knew exactly what she meant, even though the term bratty usually referred to a child. Remembering her encounter with Portia on Main Street, she could think of a more descriptive word, but, she didn't say it.

Several minutes later, Portia and her husband entered the room and sat down next to each other on a sagging wicker couch.

"I was suggesting to Trevor on the way here, that maybe we should reconsider selling Salty Cove," Portia said. "Perhaps it would be better if we keep it in the family. We could all chip in and remodel it. The property is gorgeous and the house historic, though run down." She turned to her husband and patted his knee. "But, I don't think we need to rush into any decision."

She glanced at her brother who was now sitting at an old desk sorting through papers. "Isn't that right, William? You're not in a hurry are you? Are you listening to me?"

William swung around, exchanged a look with Trevor and sighed, rather dramatically, Grace thought. "Yes, I'm listening," he said.

Bella scooted toward the edge of the sofa. "I think maybe we should leave now. William, I can give you my list."

"Portia, I think we need to sell," Trevor said, ignoring Bella. "What are we going to do with two properties? And think of all the work it would take to bring this place up to twenty first century standards. You know you like everything first- rate."

"Come on, Portia," William said, "Roone Seymoor is salivating over the possibility of owning Salty Cove. Let's strike while the iron is hot. There is some serious money to be had. We can talk about this later. I invited Bella here today to help me assess some of Mom's antique lamps and to see if she notices anything missing. Whoever he was, our thief has made a mess of things."

"Or *she* was…." Bella injected, still trying to free herself from the low couch.

"Yes, Bella, you're right," William said. "It could have been a woman. No reason at this point to exclude half the population in the investigation. Well then, maybe we should divide up the house, while we search. The police are relying on us to go through things and make a list so they can put out a bulletin."

"Do you know what time the break- in occurred?" Grace

asked.

"No. Most of us were at the funeral home last night." William glanced at Trevor.

"Are you insinuating something?" Trevor asked, eyes blazing.

William shrugged.

"William!" Portia said. "Trevor was quite ill last night. There were plenty of folks we know who weren't there. How could you even suggest such a thing?"

"I didn't suggest anything," William muttered. "Let's get on with the task at hand."

Grace remembered the crowded funeral home. Trevor hadn't been there, but neither had Mason Crawford. Even Gink had taken off. She wondered why William would make note of Trevor's absence. The Walwyn family sure had plenty of issues, and they weren't very good at concealing them.

"Let's concentrate on what we know for sure is missing," Portia said in a sullen voice. "I think we should hunt for that lamp first."

"Which lamp are you referring to?" Bella asked.

"The one that Ben probably sold to buy that fancy looking diamond Freesia Foster was flashing around at the funeral."

"I'm quite sure that was Imogene's," Bella said.

"Then it should be mine," Portia said. "William, you need to look into this. Maybe Freesia killed Ben to get the bracelet."

"I'm sure the investigators will be questioning Freesia, if they haven't already. Any one close to Ben is a potential suspect."

"Not me," Portia huffed. "In any case, I'm not convinced about selling our beloved homestead, and I won't be pushed into making a hasty decision."

"I'm the executor, and I want to get this done, and move on," William said in his courtroom voice, which had what was probably its intended effect because everyone in the room was silent for a couple of minutes. Grace had observed William in court. He could be charming and persuasive, but he was also very skillful, and she had heard him referred to as an attack dog on more than one occasion. Surely that was silly courthouse talk. At the end of the day, he hung around the local bars with cops, attorneys and the locals, like anyone else.

"We should all come to an agreement soon," Morgan said.

Portia glared at Morgan, as if to insinuate her thoughts on the matter were not appreciated. "I think it's time we spoke about the elephant in the room," Portia demanded. "Mom's special lamp."

"Not now, Portia," William warned, glancing at Grace.

"Why not?" she demanded. "It's worth a fortune, and we can't find it, can we?"

"Shut up, Portia," Trevor said. "This isn't the time."

"I thought that's what we were here for today. Isn't that why we invited Bella here? To find out more about the lamp Mom kept by her bed?"

There was an awkward silence, of the sort that made Grace feel supremely uncomfortable. Bella cleared her throat. "I do have something important to tell you all about Imogene's lamp," she said. "It's worth a lot of money. And, this is hard to say but,..."

"We know it's valuable!" Portia snorted.

"There's something you need to know about the provenance of the lamp," Bella said.

"Who cares about the provenance?" Portia said. "It's been by Mom's bedside for years. I want to know where it is now."

Bella managed to finally get out of the couch. "We've got to go," she said briskly. "We'll talk about this some other time. That said, I do remember a specific lamp that was by Imogene's bedside. If that is what you are talking about, I didn't see it today. Is it possible that she may have given it away?"

William shook his head. "No, I don't think so."

"Well, perhaps it will turn up," Bella said, handing a sheet of paper to William. "Here's my list of what lamps I did see when Grace and I were looking around earlier. "There's a very nice lamp by the Handel Company in the dining room. 'Birds of Paradise'. It has a lovely chipped ice shade that I think, if authentic, is worth a nice sum."

"Oh!" Portia exclaimed. "How much exactly?"

"I couldn't say, without a closer inspection."

"But, William, what if there is another burglary?" Portia asked.

"I've hired some temporary security," William said. "I'll take the Handel lamp home with me."

Portia was starting to object when Trevor stood up, held his hand out to Bella and nodded at Grace. "Nice seeing you again."

As Bella and Grace were escorted to the front door, it seemed to Grace that they were being hustled out as fast as possible, especially by Portia and Trevor. She figured that Portia was eager to check out the Handel. She made a mental note to ask Bella about that chipped ice shade. What in the world was that?

A crunch of stones announced the arrival of another vehicle. Cruising around the last curve of the driveway was a white, vintage Mustang convertible. The driver steered the car carefully around the potholes and slowed gently to a stop in front of the porch stairs. A young man emerged, stood by the car for half a beat, and then strode purposely toward them.

"Now who can that be?" Portia said. "Are you expecting a handyman, William?"

"No. It's probably security," William said, starting down the steps toward the visitor. "Can I help you?"

Grace froze, briefly locking eyes with the young man whose tan face, Hawaiian shirt, and deep blue eyes were shockingly like the recently deceased Ben.

"Uh oh," Bella whispered, propelling her firmly toward the Volvo. "This is going to be really interesting, but I think we better get the heck out of here."

With Bella's strong hand on her elbow, Grace looked over her shoulder to see the young man stop in front of William, a smile playing around the corners of his mouth.

"Yeah, you can help me," she heard him say. "And you can start by getting the hell off of my property."

Portia's hand flew to her mouth. Even William appeared so startled that he was momentarily silenced before demanding,

"Who do you think you are?"

"I'm Owen Walwyn, Ben's son. And you all are trespassing."

Chapter Nineteen

When Grace opened the door to Pearl's, the shop felt damp, cool, and musty, like a basement that hadn't been aired out in a very long time. The morning was dark, and she walked around turning on a few lamps and involuntarily shuddering, as she remembered last night's intruder.

Despite the physical and psychological chills Grace had been experiencing lately, she was pleased with what she saw. In the last week, the original oak floors had been scrubbed and polished, although they still revealed the marks of times gone by. The light ginger color of the walls she had painted a week ago with considerable help from Duane, were giving off a warm, luminous light. The windows, polished by Michael, were gleaming. Fresh roses rested on her table, undoubtedly a thoughtful touch from Michael. The aroma of the flowers followed her as she wandered around, looking for a place to put the finished shades she brought from home.

She glanced over to the corner where she would set up her paints so that customers could watch her construct and paint shades, and peeked in Bella's workshop, separated by a counter where she could comfortably lean on her elbows while chatting with one and all. The chandelier room, down the short hall to the back door wasn't large, since antique hanging lamps were not in great demand, but it was certainly spacious enough to house a couple of tables, a few shelves with chandelier shades and extra fabrics, trims and papers. The fairy lights alcove, a former closet with the door removed, was ready for the tiny domes that were set in glass cups, to be unpacked.

Placing her shades on a chair, Grace headed to the kitchen

where she poured herself a glass of ice water. Leaning back against the counter, she thought about her trip to Salty Cove with Bella, earlier that morning. Of course, the arrival of Owen, the spitting image of his father, had been a shock. Though not as great a shock as the one that had come a half hour later, after Bella and Grace left the Walwyn siblings speechless on the front lawn of the family home, and stopped for a cup of tea and scones at the Optimist Cafe. There, Bella had revealed what she'd known all along. Ben had a son.

"Imogene told me," she explained, "but she swore me to secrecy. The young mother in question had no desire whatsoever to spend her life with Ben. In her mind, one night of drunken misbehavior was more than enough, and she left the area. Of course, what I'm telling you is what I heard from Imogene. I never let on to Ben that I knew he had a child.

"It's obvious that Imogene didn't tell William or Portia," Grace said, masking her surprise by concentrating on buttering her scone.

"I've been stewing over this since Ben's death," Bella continued. "I had no way to find out about Owen, and I never knew his mother's name. Last night I couldn't sleep. Yesterday, I received a call from Imogene's lawyer. It appears that I am the executor for a will that Ben made a few days before he died. I'm meeting with her this afternoon."

"I wonder if Ben put Owen in his will," Grace mused. "That would explain his appearance at Salty Cove."

"Yes, it could, I suppose," Bella replied." I don't know all of the details yet. When I last saw Ben, he alluded to a surprise he had for the whole family. He said he'd found a long lost relative. My hunch, based on my last conversation with Ben, is that Owen is the heir to Salty Cove and everything in it."

"If so, then Portia and William are out of an inheritance again."

"True, but Imogene was quite generous to them. And, it's not like they have nothing. William is one of the most successful attorneys around, and Trevor is a financial advisor. Only takes on the wealthiest of clients, I'm told."

After their tea, Bella dropped Grace off in front of Pearl's saying, "I want you to be very careful. You were lucky last night. Good thing your young houseguest was with you."

Reluctantly recalling the upsetting events of the previous evening, Grace had to agree. "Before you go, what's a chipped ice shade?" she asked as she slipped out of the car.

"Chipped ice requires using fish glue and high temperatures," Bella told her. "I'll fill you in another time on the details. I've got to go. I have rather a lot to discuss with you, but I must go see the lawyer now. Incidentally, I'll have some things you can write down in that notebook of yours, which I must say, you haven't taken a single note in yet. How on earth will we solve the murder if you don't take notes?"

And, with that, she stomped on the gas pedal and shot down the street.

*****

Grace rinsed out her glass and set it on the counter. She didn't have time to worry all day about the Walwyn family and their inheritance issues if she hoped to get the shop open by tomorrow. Pausing at the end of the hallway at her office, she turned the glass knob only to find the door was stuck. She pushed against it, but it didn't budge. The fresh paint must have made it stick.

Stepping outside, she pushed her way through a tall and very wet, evergreen hedge that grew in a tight, thick border around the back of the shop, reminding herself that she needed to make time to do some light garden chores such as clipping the ungainly hedge and planting flowers in the boxes on the shop's front porch. Fall was just around the corner, but she hoped some flowers would help to catch the eye of any potential customers that might be strolling by the old building.

Grace loved natural light and knew that, once these bushes were trimmed her office would be a lot brighter. She'd put some skylights in her own cottage, and she loved looking up at the stars from her bed. Unfortunately, this train of thought had led her back to Andre and her conversation with him about her houseguest. She almost felt a little sorry for Andre, but then decided that it was time that he had a taste of what it was like to feel jealous and suspicious. And anyway, it wasn't as if they were a couple. Who did he think he was, asking all of those questions?

A dried out prickly limb scratched her as she pushed her way through the bulky hedge to her office window, swearing when a speck of blood appeared through her white linen shirtsleeve. It was, she fumed, the first time she had worn it, and now, probably the last. Everything had been going well until she thought about Andre. She paused for a moment, holding the thought of Andre and his darn note before reaching for the window sash. It was telling that neither of them had brought it up. Why was communication with this man so difficult, she wondered?

Anticipating the heft of the sash, she gave it a strong shove upwards, and when it creaked open, soot and dust falling on her damp hands, she hoisted herself up on the ledge and was just about to swing her legs inside when she felt someone's hand on her shoulder.

"Grace? What are you doing? I thought someone was trying to break in."

"William! Oh, my God! You scared me," Grace said, catching her breath. "The door to my office is stuck, so I came out here to see if I can climb in. I figured the window would be locked, but I'm in luck. It's open."

"I was on my way to my office, when I saw someone duck through the hedge," he said, pressing his way through the thick bushes. "Looks like you don't need a boost. I'll go inside and see if I can open the door for you."

Grace easily slipped through the window and into her office. Turning on the lights, she heard a peculiar, scratchy noise, and froze, listening for the sound to be repeated. Only then did she notice that her desk, neatly stacked with files when she left the shop yesterday, was a chaotic mess, and her metal filing cabinets were now leaning at a precarious angle. Boxes of carefully packaged lamps were overturned, the contents scattered around the floor, and her grandmother's carpet was rolled up against the far wall. All was quiet, until a few seconds later when William started pushing on the door from the other side muttering, "Damn painters." Grace now saw that the old fashioned latch on the inside of the door was closed. When she released it, William burst into the room.

"Isn't that strange?" she asked him. "Whoever was in here, locked the door and must have gone out the window. I don't get it."

"Makes no sense to me either," he told her. "Didn't you have construction people in here the other day? Maybe they were fooling around. It looks like…"

He broke off as a muffled, faint cry came from the rug that was rolled up against the far wall.

"Don't tell me the mice have followed me down here," Grace said, trying to make herself laugh.

"There it is again. It's coming from the rug!"

Rushing to the carpet she saw two small feet, clad in tasseled loafers, protruding from one end of the rug, while a tuft of gray brown hair extended from the other.

William swiftly unfurled the carpet.

"It's not mice," she said, "It's Michael!"

*****

As soon as Grace had removed the duct tape that covered his mouth, Michael sputtered, "I'm all right! I don't want to go the hospital!"

"I called 911," William said. "They'll be here in a couple of minutes."

Michael struggled to sit up while Grace struggled to hold him down. "Michael, please try and stay still," she said.

After a few feeble attempts to push Grace away, he finally gave up. "Where are my glasses? I must have them. I can't see a thing!"

Grace poked around until she found the glasses, still intact, and placed them carefully on Michael's nose. "Thank you, that's much better," he said. "But, really, I don't need any of those emergency people. I'm fine."

"Relax, she said. "They're here."

Chapter Twenty

After handing Grace and Beau cups of iced coffee, Duane flopped down on the floor. While she had been at the hospital with Michael, the two men had straightened the filing cabinets and cleaned up the lamp parts that had been thrown around her office, and the rug Michael had been wrapped in was now spread out in the front room. Although the coffee was cold and refreshing, Grace couldn't relax, becoming increasingly concerned about Bella's whereabouts.

Bella had said she'd be at Pearls by two-thirty, but no one had heard from her. Grace knew that she had an appointment with Ben's lawyer, but surely that was long over. She had tried Bella's cell phone and left a couple of messages, but there hadn't been any response.

"Michael seems to be okay," Grace said, pushing a damp lock of hair out of her face. "He's up and around and demanding to be released from the hospital. He's worried about his cat, Edith, being alone, even though he admitted she had plenty of food for now. The nurse said they wanted to keep him overnight, but didn't know if they'd be able to, without tying him to the bed."

"Sounds like Michael all right," Beau said. "Was he able to tell you what happened?"

"He said he didn't sleep well last night, so he decided to come to work early this morning. 'Get a jump on the day,' he said. Someone grabbed him from behind when he was opening the front door and blindfolded him. Then his arms were tied behind his back, and he was taken to my office. The intruder interrogated him about the whereabouts of a lamp. He said it was valuable and had dragonflies on it. When Michael told him he didn't know what he was talking about, the man got increasingly angry with him. Michael said he figured he had nothing to lose, so when he perceived that the intruder was mulling over what he might do next, he launched himself at him, hoping to knock him over and, in Michael's words, 'stomp on him.' Although he put up again, in Michael's words, a 'ferocious struggle,' the man, who was much larger and stronger, picked him up and rolled him in the carpet."

"Wow!" said Duane.

Then the man gagged him, locked the office door, and went out the window. But, not before threatening him with far worse if he found out that Michael had misled him."

"Wow!" Duane said again.

"And that's not all," Grace said, chewing on a piece of ice from her coffee, before filling them in on her encounter with an intruder in the shop. Beau and Duane wanted to make a plan to have someone in the building at all times. It was decided that Beau would stay in the bookstore tonight, and Duane would take over for him tomorrow. Like all good bookstores, Beaus Books had at least two comfy reading chairs that would make their nights comfortable.

"According to Michael," Grace continued. "If this person doesn't find what he's looking for, he'll be making another visit to Pearl's. And soon."

During the rest of the afternoon, Grace periodically telephoned Bella, only to continue to get her voice mail. In the meantime, she set up her desk and filled her old metal filing cabinet with folders of paperwork pertaining to the business. Her desk was large, one of those old 1950's schoolteachers' desks that popped up every now and then in thrift stores. There was no room in her budget for new furniture. And, anyway, she loved the expanse of oak surface, nicked and scratched with the blotches and scribbling of students, or maybe even teachers, who had marked their passage through their school years. If only the furniture could talk, Grace thought. If only it could tell her what had happened to Michael. His story was strange indeed. A man looking for a dragonfly lamp, or was it a dragonfly shade? Perhaps the man was mentally ill. A mentally ill man resorting to violence to find a dragonfly lamp was an alarming thought. But what was truly frightening was the threat he made to return until he got what he wanted.

"Duane, why don't we close up now?" she said, finally. "You've been a great help today."

"Okay Ms. Tolliver. Maybe I'll go see if Beau needs anything. You should see it up there. He's got hundreds, maybe thousands of books all over the place, and he's kind of slow when it comes to organizing them. I tried to tell him that if he keeps reading through every book before he shelves it, he's never gonna get done."

"You might try reading one every now and then yourself," Grace suggested.

"Beau's just like you. Always trying to get me to read something. He's said he's got some detective books I might like, as soon as he can locate them in the mess. But, I don't know. I never really liked detectives. They were always arresting me. I'm not talking about Detective Cruz, of course, because..."

"Yes, I understand." Grace said, remembering Duane's unhappy experience with the detective last winter.

"Because we're friends now," Duane continued.

"Really?"

Duane often referred to people, even those he hardly knew, as friends, but she was taken by surprise when Duane said, "I house sat for him the other night when he was at a conference. All I had to do was feed and walk the dogs. I had the whole place to myself. He's got a super surround sound system. It was awesome. His partner, Emma, asked me to go by her place and feed her bird, too. And, they paid me!"

"Emma's bird?"

"Yeah. Emma's at the conference, too. Petey is pretty cute, but he doesn't do much except hop around his cage. Not like Andre's dogs. Lola and Frank are a lot of fun. And they like me. Not sure if Petey likes me or not, come to think of it."

"Hmmm, well that *is* interesting," Grace said. Until now,

she had thought that Andre and Duane's relationship was one of mutual wariness, and since Duane didn't ordinarily consider police officers his "friends," she was stunned to hear that the two had been in touch with one another. For Andre to entrust his beloved dogs with Duane was almost beyond belief.

"Okay, let's get out of here," she said. "I really can't concentrate anyway because I'm worried about Bella. I'm going to go to her house and have another look. She had an appointment with a lawyer, but I just called her office, and the assistant told me Bella had left hours ago."

"Should I go with you?" Duane asked.

"No. I know where she keeps her key. I'll let myself into her house if I need to. After all, she might be sleeping. If everything is all right with her, I'll go back to the hospital to check in on Michael. That is if he hasn't escaped yet."

The thought of Michael hanging from a hospital window clinging to a bed sheet made Grace smile, but the knot in her stomach made sure she wasn't distracted for long.

Chapter Twenty-One

Finding Bella's front door locked and no answer to her doorbell, Grace circled the house. A squirrel scampered up a tree and a cardinal perched in the top branches of a maple tree, announced her arrival to the neighborhood birds.

Gaining entry through the unlocked back entry, Grace hurried from room to cluttered room of the small saltbox house, calling Bella's name.

Deciding to go upstairs in order to make a thorough search, Grace went so far as to check closets and under beds before looking in the bathroom.

The first thing that Grace noticed was that the shampoo bottle and soap dish were on the floor. At the far end under the window was an old claw foot tub, filled to the brim with towels and a flowered bedspread. The window was open, and a stiff breeze was stirring the curtains. Grace picked up the shampoo and soap dish, most likely knocked over by the wind, and placed them on the counter next to the sink, and opened the door to the shower stall, even though she could see through the diffused glass, that it was empty.

Finding nothing out of the ordinary, she was about to go downstairs to check the basement and garage, when she heard a muffled cry coming from the direction of the tub.

Her heart pounding, she pulled back the towels and spread. "Oh my God," she cried. "Bella!"

Tied up, gagged, and looking every one of her eighty-five years, Bella, her eyes filled with tears, stared up at Grace.

"I thought I was a goner," Bella gasped, once Grace had gently pulled the tape away from her mouth. "You've got to help me find Ben's killer now!"

Chapter Twenty-Two

Wondering if she had ever been this angry, Grace sat in the emergency room waiting for a nurse or doctor to let her see Bella. She was frightened, and confused, too, but most of all, she was positively steamed. That someone would dare attack Michael and Bella was so startling, so inconceivable, and so wrong, her mind raced with a multitude of questions that she didn't know the answer to. There was no question now she would help Bella find out what had happened to Ben. A line had been crossed and there was no going back. Whatever she needed to do, she would do.

What she couldn't wrap her mind around was Bella's asking for her help meant that Bella believed her attacker, searching for a lamp, might have something to do with Ben's murder. But why would anyone attack Bella and Michael?

Grace was getting a headache. As she closed her eyes and rubbed her throbbing temples, she repeated to herself her new mantra. 'A line had been crossed and there is no going back. I *will* get to the bottom of this. No matter what.'

Chapter Twenty-Three

It was past midnight when Grace parked her car in her barn, inhaling the sweet scent of honeysuckle from the vines that clung to the shingles and pitched roof. Glancing at the quarter moon, a few misty stars, and the dark marsh, she thought how good it felt to be home. Exhausted, but relieved that Michael and Bella were safe for now in Cape Cod Hospital, she took a deep breath of salty air and listened to the chirping of katydids. Last spring, she had installed safety lighting around her house and as she approached, a motion light illuminated her flagstone patio. She saw a still figure that she was fairly certain must be Felix. He probably locked himself out of the house and had decided to stretch out on her lounge chair. But, no point in being careless, she thought, as she bent to pick up a rake that was laying at the edge of her vegetable garden.

Holding her breath, she stepped lightly across the few feet of damp lawn to the edge of her patio. She hesitated beside the chair for a moment and then, as her eyes adjusted to the shadows, saw that it was Andre. What on earth, she wondered, was he doing on her lounge chair in the middle of the night? He looked so peaceful, breathing softly, mumbling in his sleep. It was a shame to wake him, but she did, giving the chair a whack with her rake and declaring, "Fine watchman you'd make."

Andre jumped. "Mierda, Gracie! I wasn't asleep. I was just resting my eyes for a minute," he exclaimed, pushing up on one elbow and drawing a hand through his hair.

"Good thing you have that gun, but, if I had one too, and I were a very bad person, you'd be dead by now," Grace told him.

Andre reached down to the ground and touched the Glock

that was tucked underneath the chair. He gave her a chagrined smile and pulled her down to sit beside him. She noticed that he was serious now, although, as always, smiling or not, his dimple was visible.

"I heard about Michael and Bella," he said. "Are they going to be all right? Are you okay?"

Grace nodded. "Bella and Michael will be all right," she said, "and I'm okay, too."

"Fill me in on what's happening."

"Come on inside. I have some iced tea. Want some?"

"Yeah, sure. On second thought, do you have any coffee?" Andre asked, following her into the kitchen.

Grace picked up her pot and removed the lid. "I guess my houseguest left some. It's stale. I'll make a fresh pot."

Andre took the pot from her hand, took a cup from her cabinet, poured coffee in it and thrust it into the microwave.

"By the way, where is your houseguest?" he asked. "I've been here quite a while and I haven't seen anyone. There's no one in your guestroom."

Grace filled a tall glass to the brim with ice and poured in a brew of tea for herself. "You've been snooping around, have you?" she said accusingly.

"I had to secure the house, what with everything that's going on around here," Andre replied, but she caught the twinkle in his green eyes. "I hope you don't mind. You forgot to close your living room window."

"I didn't forget. No doubt, my houseguest did," Grace told him, considering the distinct possibility that Felix's days were numbered.

"So, where is he?"

"I have no idea. Maybe he's working out at the gym," Grace fibbed. Although the thought of Felix, working out was so incongruous, that she almost laughed. "He might have even come and gone while you were napping on my patio. I don't keep tabs on him. There are more important things on my mind."

Andre shrugged. "I still find it hard to believe that you

would have a man you know absolutely nothing about stay with you."

"It's really none of your business," Grace said, realizing that she was probably taking some of her anger toward Felix out on him. She also recognized that she wasn't *that* unhappy with his concern.

Andre took a sip of coffee. "God awful, weak stuff," he complained. "The guy can't even make coffee." He dumped the remaining coffee into her sink. "But, you're right, it's none of my business. So, tell me everything you can remember about what happened today."

Grace related to Andre the day's events. How she and William discovered Michael wrapped in her grandmother's Persian rug. Michael was doing fine she assured him, but the hospital insisted he stay overnight so they could monitor his elevated blood pressure. Bella was sedated and, hopefully, sleeping by now.

"According to Michael, a man sneaked up on him at Pearl's, demanding to know the whereabouts of a lamp. A lamp with dragonflies," she continued. "Michael had no idea what he was talking about. He couldn't reason with the man, and when he had the chance, he tried a surprise attack, but was overpowered, and threatened with a return visit if this person found out that Michael had been holding out on him."

"Who is William?"

"William Walwyn. Ben's brother."

Andre nodded. "Yes, of course."

"His office is only a block away. Bella and I saw him earlier in the day at Salty Cove. He may have been on his way back to work. At any rate, Michael told me that Sophie, the daughter of the owners of the Beach Sparrow Inn, who frequently stops by to visit, might have seen something. He saw her across the street when he first arrived at the store."

By this time, Andre was busy taking notes.

"Later, when I couldn't reach Bella by phone, I went over to her house," Grace told him. "When she didn't answer her door, I let myself in, and after searching the house, found her in the claw foot tub. Her doctor said she'll be fine after a few days of rest. She was very shook up, of course. Poor Bella, she must have been terrified. I'm sure Michael was frightened as well, but, of course, he won't admit it."

When she wiped away a tear, Andre put an arm around her and drew her close, and said in a low voice, "I'm so sorry this has happened. I know how much you love Bella and Michael."

"I do love them, and worry about them," she admitted, leaning against his warmth and enjoying the familiar Andre scent, crisp, with a hint of salt and sea. And then, remembering that things between them were not what they once were, she pulled herself away. Had she lost her mind? It had been a difficult day and she was exhausted. Did that explain why she was in Andre's arms? The last thing she remembered was sipping from her ice tea and leaning against her kitchen counter.

Andre relaxed his arm and took a step away from her. His movement was unhurried, and he continued the conversation as if nothing out of the ordinary had happened.

"Did you have a chance to talk to Bella?" Andre asked. Now he appeared to be all business, the police officer on a case.

Grace dabbed at her eyes with a tissue. "Bella told me that when she opened her back door, someone came up behind her, blindfolded her, led her into the kitchen, and started to berate her about the whereabouts of a valuable lamp. This man seemed sure that Bella was holding out on him, even though she repeatedly told him that she didn't know what he was talking about. He led her through the house, into every room, threatening to kill her if she didn't tell them where the lamp was. And then..."

Grace hesitated and Andre looked up from his notes. Their eyes met for a few seconds.

"And then...," she continued, "he put duct tape over her mouth and put her in the claw foot tub. He said he'd be back, and she better have the dragonfly lamp waiting for him."

Andre put down his notebook. "Did they injure her in any way?" he asked. "Other than what you've told me?"

"No. But her hands and feet were bound, and she suffered

some pretty nasty looking abrasions."

Andre paced back and forth, from one end of her kitchen to another. "As you know, the local cops are investigating. But I'm disturbed about what happened today, and I want to know as much as possible. Do you know anything about a so- called dragonfly lamp?"

"No, and Michael told me that he had no idea what the man was talking about either."

"What about Bella? Did she say anything specific about the lamp?"

Before Grace could answer, Andre got a text.

"A thrift store in Hyannis was held up. Might be a connection. An employee reported that she worked late, then closed up at about eight- thirty," he told her. "That was a little more than three hours ago."

"Could be connected, I guess. Thrift stores often sell antique lighting, if that's what this person is looking for."

It's possible," Andre said. "In any case, I have some questions for you regarding the murder. Let's go over that, too."

Grace was surprised to realize how relieved she was that whatever had happened in Hyannis did not, apparently, require his presence.

"Ben Walwyn inherited the estate known as Salty Cove," Andre said. "Shortly thereafter, someone shoots him and he falls into his swimming pool. So, the obvious question is why? Who would gain by Ben's death? From what I know so far, it would appear that his siblings William and Portia are the sole benefactors. Correct? So obviously William and Portia would be suspects, but there may be others as well. Ben was an accomplished swimmer and archer and gave lessons. Maybe a former student had a beef with him."

"Sure, but from what I've heard about Ben, he had problems with a lot of people," Grace said. "What you may not know is that some things have changed since this morning. Bella and I were out at Salty Cove, and when we were leaving, a white mustang convertible pulled up the driveway. A younger version of Ben stepped out, scaring the you know what out of everyone, and said he's Ben's son, Owen."

Andre let out a low whistle. "So, I guess if this Owen is who he says he is, he might inherit. Or, then again, that would depend on Ben having made a will. In fact, I think Gelb is supposed to be checking that out today."

"Maybe he did, and we'll find out soon," Grace replied, deciding not to disclose the fact that Bella had known about Owen and was the executor of the will. After all, she didn't want to betray Bella's confidence, and she knew the truth, whatever it was, would come out soon.

"William asked Bella to come to the house to help him see what might be missing after it was broken into the night of Ben's wake," she went on. "He said he wanted her to look at some other lamps that he thought might have some value."

"So why were you there? C'mon Grace. I hope you're not getting involved in this."

"Of course not. I told you, I don't want anything to do with Ben's murder investigation. I went with Bella, because she wanted company."

Grace knew that it was definitely not a good idea to tell him that Bella had asked her to help find out who was responsible for Ben's death.

Andre sighed. "Don't hold out on me, Grace. I'm here because you are in danger. Michael and Bella are lucky to be alive."

How was it that he always seemed to know that she might not be sharing everything with him? Grace wondered. Was she so obvious? But he was right about today's traumatic events.

"Did you and Bella find anything missing, or anything of value out there?"

"Bella thought a Handel might be worth thousands of dollars."

"What's a Handel?"

"Handel was a company that produced lamps around the same time as the well-known Tiffany Studios. They made lovely lamps."

"Okay. Do you have any idea about anyone else, besides the

family, who might know anything about a valuable lamp that might have been at Salty Cove?"

"I suppose there a number of people that might know about it," Grace tried to suppress a yawn. "Sorry, I think I've got to get some rest, but, I'm sure Imogene had friends and neighbors who might know something."

"Why don't you go to sleep? I'll camp out on the loveseat for a while. You shouldn't be alone."

For once, Grace didn't find herself ready to argue with Andre. When she awoke at dawn, she watched as he backed his car out of her driveway and drove off in the direction of Main Street. The fact that she had slept soundly was due in good part to knowing that he was with her.

But, because such thoughts were unsettling, she swept them away and began the day.

Chapter Twenty-Four

Grace arrived at the hospital at seven-thirty, as doctors were making their morning rounds, and hot breakfasts were delivered to patients.

A young man sprawled on a chair in the hallway, asleep, his head back, his mouth hanging open, and his long legs stretch out into the hallway.

"Duane!" Grace sputtered. "What on earth...?"

"Duane straggled to his feet. "Hey, Ms. Tolliver. I guess you're wondering what I'm doing here."

"Well, I am surprised."

"After I left the shop, I went around to Michael's, let myself in, fed Edith her dinner of chunky tuna, gave her water and a few pets and then went to Emma's house to feed Petey and clean his cage. But after I got your text, I was feeling kind of nervous. I couldn't stop thinking about Michael and Bella. So, I decided to come here and watch over them."

"You are so sweet and thoughtful," Grace said, and then a thought occurred to her. "I didn't know you had a key to Michael's house."

"I don't actually. I had to fiddle with the... well, I just figured out a way. I do have some past experience breaking into..."

Grace cut him off. "I don't even want to know. Let's check on Bella first, shall we?"

Bella was sitting up in bed her hair rumpled, her glasses askew, staring down at her breakfast tray with an expression of distaste. "Now what do you suppose that is?" she asked pointing at a mushy white substance that was nestled next to a soft boiled egg.

"I don't know, but that bagel looks good," Duane said.

Handing her bagel to Duane, Bella said, "What are you folks doing here, so early in the morning?"

"Duane was so concerned about you he spent the night in a chair outside your room," Grace told her.

"Imagine that!" Bella put her hand on her chest. "Thank you, Duane. Would you like this pat of butter for your bagel?"

"You're welcome, Captain Bella. Yup, I'll have some butter. Got any jam?"

There was a soft knock on the door, and Michael ambled in, fully dressed, his hair combed, his bowtie in place. "Good morning, everyone," he said.

"It's such a relief to see both of you." Grace said." How are you feeling, Bella?"

"Pretty darn good. The doc says I can go home if I want. My wrists hurt me some, but I'm certainly a lot better than I was in that tub. I thought I was going to die. Thank you for saving me, Grace," she added, dabbing at her eyes with her napkin.

Grace leaned over Bella's bed and gave her a hug. When she did the same to Michael, she saw his cheeks turn pink. She knew that he believed hugging had become far too commonplace among friends, and that he put up with her occasional displays of affection, because he assumed that her years living in California were to blame for her lack of decorum, and that these kinds of habits were hard to break.

There was another knock at Bella's door. "I thought we were the early birds," William said, as he stepped aside to let Portia, Trevor, and Morgan in. Portia immediately rushed over to Bella's bedside, while Michael thanked William him for his efforts to help save him at the lamp shop.

"We've all been so frightened," Portia said. "What a terrible thing to happen to you."

Bella waved her away. "I'm really quite all right, Portia. I haven't been awake long enough to sift through everything that happened yesterday, but I expect I'll get through it. One does, you know. I think I'm going to be released today."

"You must come to our house," Portia said. "Isn't that right, Trevor?"

Trevor, who wore a stylish business suit, stuck his finger in his shirt collar and ran it around as if it was too tight. "Yes, of course, you shouldn't be alone."

William moved swiftly to the other side of Bella's bed. "We have plenty of room at our house," he said. "You can have the guest bedroom with the view of the bay. Wouldn't that be lovely?"

"We insist," Morgan told her. "And, that's that."

There was a babble of argument, that didn't let up until Bella waved her arms for silence, letting the competing offers hang in the air like the odor wafting from her breakfast tray.

"No," Michael told them with what appeared to Grace to be a deliberate attempt to stop any further discussion. "It's already been decided. Bella is coming to my house. We'll keep an eye on each other. It will be the easiest and best thing."

Everyone in the crowded hospital room looked at Bella. "Thank you all," she said firmly, but I will stay with Michael."

It seemed to Grace that Bella's decision left more than a couple of people in the room uncomfortable, and she had to admit to herself, that she was one of them. First of all, it seemed too early for them to leave the hospital after such traumatic events, and the plan they'd worked out to stay together didn't seem to be a safe one. But everyone knew that when Bella set her mind to something, it was useless to try to persuade her otherwise.

Grace decided it was time to leave Bella and Michael and get to Pearl's. It was still early, but there was so much to do, and she expected that more customers might stop by today to see the improvements in the shop. After sending Duane home to catch up on his sleep, she blew Bella a kiss, and lingering in the doorway watched as William and Portia grabbed the empty chairs, and pulled them close to Bella's bed. Morgan stood stiffly behind William her arms crossed and her lips pressed. Trevor, after checking his watch, said he would be going as well, as he also had a busy day ahead. Nodding to all of them, he headed in the direction of the elevators.

"Bella, I'm sorry about what happened to you. I can't imagine how scared you must have been," Portia said, patting Bella's hand, and glancing at William. "There's no explanation other than a lunatic is on the loose. I hope the police find him soon."

"Can you recall anything more about your attacker?" William asked. "Perhaps his voice or his height."

"I couldn't really tell. I know that sounds strange, but..."

"Not at all Bella," William assured her. "The memory can be severely tried after such a traumatic event. Don't worry, you'll probably remember more in the days ahead. And you must be reeling, as we are, from the shock of that imposter who calls himself Owen, claiming to be Ben's son."

"We think he's a fraud," Portia added.

Grace's heart skipped a beat, as she wondered what, if anything Bella might reveal about Owen. But Bella shrugged noncommittally and yawned in such an exaggerated way that it was clear that she wanted some, or perhaps all, of her visitors to leave. "Thank you for coming to see me. I need to get a little rest now before I'm released. I'll be all right, don't worry," she added "Michael will take good care of me and I of him."

*****

When Grace saw Michael duck back to his room, she followed him. "Are you sure you two are going to be all right?" Grace asked. "It doesn't sound like you will be very safe all by yourselves."

"On the contrary. We'll be very secure." Michael assured her. "We're going to have our own private security."

"Really? That's a good idea, I should have thought of that myself."

"Not to worry. Detective Cruz stopped by early this morning. He thinks it best if we stay together. He'll be bunking on my couch, so we'll be plenty protected."

As she headed down the corridor, Grace felt a sudden pull on her heart and wondered who would sleep on her couch and keep her safe?

Chapter Twenty-Five

The village was peaceful and sleepy on this warm, sunny Monday morning, but inside Pearl's it was as cool as November, because, in the course of yesterday's commotion, the new window air conditioners had been left on. She went from room to room to turn them down, and seeing the sun cheerfully filtering through the windows, it was hard to believe that such a terrible event occurred here less than twenty-four hours ago. She realized that it was going to be hard to shake the frightening feelings that now threatened to overcome her.

When the bell on the front door rang, Grace hustled out to see who it was. She tried to hide her disappointment when she saw Clay.

"Where is everyone?" he said. "I thought this was your re-opening day. I expected to see all of you bright and early, with coffee and goodies to welcome returning customers. Maybe there is something in the kitchen?" Clay said, taking off his straw hat and heading down the hall. "It certainly is chilly in here," he complained.

"I guess you haven't heard. Michael and Bella are in the hospital," Grace told him. She couldn't help but notice that for the first time in her recollection, she knew something that Clay didn't.

Coming to a quick stop, he removed his sunglasses and stared at her with his bird- like eyes. "Are they sick? I've heard there's a new restaurant on the highway that is causing some stomach issues."

"No, they're not sick." Grace wasn't keen on sharing all of yesterday's events with Clay, but she knew she would have to fill him in on most of what had happened. Besides, Bella and Michael had put up with him for so many years that he was almost, albeit, *a big almost*, their friend. She knew that Clay would rush about, telling everyone he encountered the remarkable story. So, it was better if he got his facts straight, even though she knew that whatever Clay passed on would be greatly embellished.

"My Goodness," he said, fanning himself with his hat, despite the chill. "Someone looking for a lamp? Surely it has to be a disturbed person. What kind of lamp were they looking for?"

"I don't know all of the details," Grace lied. She was sure the police were keeping most aspects of the investigation as quiet as possible in the small village.

"But, Grace, you must find out," Clay persisted. "The details are the important thing, after all. And what will you do without Michael and Bella? Who will make brownies?"

"Duane will help me."

"Duane? You can't be serious."

He sat down slowly in the chintz-covered armchair. Clay could never reconcile himself to the idea that Grace now employed Duane Kerbey, a former drug addict. Despite all that happened in the previous year and all the growth Duane had demonstrated, it would never be enough for Clay. But Grace knew a secret about him. A few years back, he had been busted during a raid on a house in Yarmouth and arrested for cocaine possession. The charges had been dismissed because there were bigger fish to fry in that bust, but Clay liked to act like he was better than everyone else on the planet. Grace knew he was a hypocrite and he would never change.

After contemplating the news, Clay pulled himself nimbly out of the chair. "I hope you don't mind, but I need one of these," he said as he vigorously unscrewed a bulb from a lamp. "And don't scowl like that, Grace, you have dozens of these." And without another word he dropped the bulb in his jacket pocket and glided swiftly out of the shop.

When Duane arrived sometime after lunch, Grace told him

that after Clay had spread the word about Michael and Bella, it seemed that most of the downtown populace had rushed to Pearl's. Most everyone had been very kind and offered all kinds of help, all of which she had declined with many thanks. But, there were others, she surmised, who were merely curious and left before they might feel obliged to lend a hand.

Even her dad and Gink had dropped in. By the time Grace had been able to separate herself from a customer who was ordering a complicated handmade pleated shade, and waited on another who wanted her to show him a Victorian pressed pattern oil lamp, they had left. Somehow, in all of the commotion, she had managed to sell a couple of matching cylinder lamps with a leaf motif, and two shades made from fabric covered with red polka dots.

Duane got busy right away completing the work he had started yesterday, checking wires and vacuuming glass from her office floor, putting right what the intruder had so forcefully put wrong. He even got her computer up and running, which was one of many surprising things about Duane. He seemed to have a natural ability to fix things.

"Where did you learn about computers?" she asked him.

"I took a class in jail. My teacher said I had an attitude."

Grace rubbed her chin. "Do you mean aptitude?"

Duane nodded. "Yeah, like I said."

Michael's freshly painted shelves were ready for the shades to be stacked. It was amazing what a transformation had taken place. Of course, Pearl's would always be Pearl's. No matter how hard she and the others tried to bring order, the shop seemed to be on the verge of chaos. Lamps were stacked in the oddest of places waiting for their owners to come and get them, delivery boxes often cluttered the floors, and Bella's workspace was a cyclone of parts, tools and cords. Grace was well aware that the genial mess of the shop was cherished by most of her customers, and that it wouldn't do to make things too orderly and new. They might well enjoy the improvements, but they also wanted to feel at home at Pearl's.

Tonight, she would stay late and by tomorrow, the shop

would be almost back to normal. But, of course, there was no normal without Bella and Michael. She hoped that they would take some time to rest up. She selfishly wished that neither of them would retire, but at their age, it was a possibility and constantly at the back of her mind.

"Do you think we can hang the chandeliers today?" she asked Duane.

"Just me and you? Maybe, but I think some of them are too large for you."

"Well, Bella and Michael can't do it. Let's see how far we get."

The rest of the afternoon, Grace spent with Duane in the chandelier room, atop Michael's ladder. Somehow, they managed with grit and determination to swing several large pieces into place. Grace flicked on the light switch, and together they watched the lights play on the upper reaches of the room from the bare bulb styles. Diffused light spilled out of the chandeliers with shades.

"Wow!" Duane exclaimed.

"It's gorgeous!" Grace said with excitement. "Duane, we did it!"

"We did, Ms. Tolliver." Duane slapped her hand with a high five. "Very cool."

"I really appreciate your hard work, Duane. It looks like I may have to rely on you more that I had originally thought. Are you happy here?"

"Yup. I am. I think I'm getting the hang of things now. I know I'm a slow learner and you've been really nice to me."

"Many people are slow learners when they start something new," Grace assured him. "I'm very impressed that you show up every day, ready to work. After we get through the remodel, let's sit down and talk. I think maybe a raise is in store for you."

"Cool. I never had a raise before."

"You've never had a job before," Grace said.

*****

Duane, needing a break and craving a snack, went off to get

ice cream. A man with rusty colored hair, wearing dark glasses with round black frames, sauntered into the store, and Grace instantly recognized him as, Roone Seymoor, the neighbor of Salty Cove, who seemed to be intent on purchasing the property from William and Portia. She wondered if he knew anything about Owen and the sudden possible change in ownership.

He was dressed casually in a blue cotton shirt and tan slacks, and boat shoes without socks. Sweeping the shades off his face, he appraised the room before turning his attention on Grace.

"Very nice. I like what you've done around here," he said finally, with a disarming smile. "The former owners would be shocked of course."

Grace laughed. Was he flirting with her? She wasn't sure why she felt that way, but she definitely felt like he might be. "Everyone likes to put their own stamp on things," she said. "Matt & Milo are in Florida now, sort of enjoying retirement, but threatening to return to the Cape."

"The Cape is a hard place to leave," he agreed. "I've only been here for three years. That's very short in Cape Cod time. For most longtime residents, it's as if I just arrived yesterday afternoon. Now, that I've found paradise, I couldn't imagine leaving. By the way, we've never been properly introduced. I'm Roone Seymoor," he added, extending a smooth hand. "Nice to see you again. How is your bird faring?"

"I'm Grace Tolliver," she said. "I bought Pearl's about a year ago. The osprey is fine, thanks to your intervention. I don't remember seeing you in the shop, but obviously you've been here before today."

"Yes. I come by every now and then to see Bella. I have a collection of antiques, including lighting, and Bella is so knowledgeable that I would never purchase any lamp without her advice. In fact, I left a lamp for repair with her a week ago."

"Yes, the floor lamp. It's such an interesting piece of craftsmanship. We're a little behind at the moment. Were you promised it would be ready today?" Grace asked.

"No, Bella never promises anything. When it's done, it's done. I've come to realize that she has her own schedule." He took a step closer and speaking softly said, "I heard about what happened to Bella and Michael. I'm so sorry. Are they going to be all right?"

"I certainly hope so," Grace said.

"We've started a neighborhood watch in our area," he went on. "We're all a bit scared. It's a shame to have to consider it, but it's the way things are now. Do you know anything about the police investigation of Ben's murder? We're all anxious to have this cleared up as soon as possible."

"No, I don't," Grace said, not that she'd tell him if she did.

"My wife, Julia, and I became friendly with Imogene in the past year," he said, by way of explanation. "She was a very nice woman. We tried to help her out. Ben wasn't always the most responsible caretaker, if you know what I mean. Occasionally, we'd stop by and visit, bring her fresh flowers or other treats from the market. In the end, she was confined to her bedroom, so we would take them up to her, and sit awhile." Leaning forward, he said, "I heard about someone claiming to be Ben's son has appeared out of nowhere."

"Oh, really?" Grace was amazed, as always, at how fast news traveled on Cape Cod.

"Yes. I imagine he might inherit Salty Cove," Roone said. "I'm concerned because my property overlooks the place."

"I don't know anything about the situation at Salty Cove," Grace fibbed. It was obvious he was trying to pump her for some inside information, but she wasn't going to give him any.

"Ah, of course," Roone said, behind a smile that belied any disappointment that he may have felt. "Now that I'm here, I might as well take a look and see what you might have acquired since my last visit. Is it okay with you if I wander around a bit?"

"Yes, wander away. I'll be at my worktable if you need me," Grace said, wondering, as she had before, if Roone had seen her at the funeral home and noted that there seemed to be something flirtatious in his manner. Wasn't he married to the attractive woman dressed in black who was standing near the casket at the wake? Julia wasn't it? And wasn't he already flirting with the other woman, another neighbor? Roone appeared to be one busy guy. A rather sexy, busy guy, Grace couldn't help but think.

A woman dressed in a pale blue linen sleeveless dress, gold bracelets clinking on her arm and carrying a large straw purse, entered the shop. With no more than a glance at Grace, she sauntered over to where Roone was holding a lamp in the air, scrutinizing it up close, apparently checking the seams. He didn't appear to be aware of the woman, who Grace now recognized, as that very same woman from the funeral home, Luna.

When he did see her, Roone almost dropped the lamp, and when she smiled at him and snuggled next to his shoulder, he responded with a tight smile and took a step away from her.

"Are you crazy?" Grace heard him hiss. "Not here!" Luna frowned, and slipped around the table, where she began looking through a display of finials.

Roone approached Grace at her table where she was setting up a shade to be painted. "This is very nice," he said to Grace, holding a pale green jade carved lamp. "I'll take it. Can you gift wrap it for me?"

Grace was happy about the sale, not a big one, but a sale nonetheless. When Roone had asked about gift wrapping, she inwardly groaned. Michael could make year old newspaper with coffee stains look special. She didn't have this talent herself. Her friends and family often laughed at her attempts to wrap presents. She carried the lamp to Michael's gift-wrap table and was going through some paper selections when her cell rang.

"Hi, I wanted to call earlier, but I had to finish a report that was due in court tomorrow," Audrey said. "Judge had to have it immediately. You remember those days. How are Michael and Bella?"

"They're all right, but I'm still worried about them," Grace told her. "It was such a shock. Listen, I'm kind of busy now. Can I call you back?"

"What are you doing?"

"I'm gift wrapping a present for a customer."

"Gift wrapping?" Audrey laughed. "I hope they're not too picky."

"I don't know for sure, but I'm afraid he might be. I've got to go."

"Want to meet at the Tavern for dinner? We can sit outside. Just say yes or no and I'll hang up."

Grace hesitated for half a second than said, "Yes. Seven-thirty."

She'd been wrapping while talking to Audrey and the package looked shoddier than even she could have imagined. The ribbon was too short, pieces of tape were hanging off the sides, and she'd ripped, ever so slightly, a corner of the paper. It was amazing that she was so bad at this. After all, she was careful, creative, and neat when she worked on her shades.

"I'm sorry," she said to Roone, as she placed the gift on the counter. Luna had joined him and was nonchalantly stroking his arm, as if he wasn't already married to someone else. "This is really not my best effort. If you like, I can try again or you could bring it back and...."

Roone shifted away from Luna and lifted the package. "No," he said, as the bow slid off. "It's fine. Charming. Thank you so much, and it was a pleasure to meet you."

As they left, Luna waved her fingers in a friendly goodbye.

*****

Twenty minutes later, as Grace was intently gluing trim to a shade, another task that Michael did effortlessly, Clay rushed in the door.

"Grace!" he shouted as if she wasn't a mere ten feet away.

"I've got the most fabulous news," he told her. "You're going to be indebted to me forever."

That didn't sound like good news to Grace, who eyed him warily, her fingers wrapped around the shade holding glue in place.

"I just got back from Falmouth. Remember the old inn that was closed for a number of years? The one with the exceptional property and view?"

"I really don't know what you're talking about."

"Well, you should know, everyone does," he said frowning.

"It's been bought by ambitious new owners and is in the midst of a major re-do. They have a decorator on their staff, of course. She's here for the next few days, making sketches and that sort of thing. They brought her in from New York City. She's very sophisticated, dressed head to toe in black. Lots of silver jewelry." Clay paused to catch his breath. "I dropped in on her, and hinted that she might take me on as a consultant since I know everything about Cape Cod style."

"That's nice, Clay," Grace replied. "But I don't see what this has to do with me."

"You're going to love this, Grace." Grace shuddered as she contemplated Clay using her name and love in the same sentence. "I told her about your shop," he explained. "And she's most interested in having as much as possible locally made. Or in her words, 'sourced.' She will need oodles of your handmade shades. Are you excited now?"

Grace gasped. It did sound exciting. "Are you sure? What do you mean by oodles?"

"Um, I think around twenty and maybe more. She wants to meet with you right away and would like you to call her and set up a time to come and talk."

"It sounds wonderful and I'd like to meet her, but I have no staff at the moment," Grace said, overcome by a combination of exhilaration and frustration. It would be such a great opportunity. Maybe word would spread to other inns, and then, maybe, more opportunities would come her way. "I suppose it might be possible if she's not in a hurry, and Michael and Bella don't retire after yesterday's ordeal. And, of course, it would depend on what type of shades she needs and if there is any hand painting, or other kind of special request involved."

"She's in a big hurry," Clay told her. "These are important people. They're always in a rush. She's from New York City! I promised her you'd be able to get them done in ten days."

Grace rose and confronted him angrily. "What are you thinking?" she demanded. "Even if everyone were here, it would be very difficult to get a project of that size done in that time frame. Why did you take it upon yourself to promise her anything?"

"I had to," he protested. "I wanted you to get the job, of course. Really, Grace, you've got to think outside the box. Couldn't you hire some more criminals like Duane and teach them what to do?"

"I'm beginning to wonder why you're so interested in this anyway." Grace said, ignoring his sarcasm.

"Obviously, I'll get a very nice commission and she will see that I can deliver when dealing with the natives."

Grace sighed. "Give me her name and number."

"Will you call her?"

"Yes, I'll call her. But don't spend your commission yet."

*****

When Duane returned, with a chocolate cone for her, Grace had just finished arranging a collection of miniature lamps in her window. Popularly known as "mini's, they burned oil and were used for practical and decorative purposes. Like the candle burning Fairy lamps, their glow didn't last long, but long enough for someone to fall asleep, or, as Bella liked to say, allow enough time for some hanky-panky.

"Will Bella and Michael be back soon?" Duane asked.

"I hope so, but I don't really know. We'll have to take things day by day for now."

"Okay, don't worry. I've got your back."

"Thanks, I appreciate that," she said, surprised to find that she really did.

Chapter Twenty-Six

Audrey was sitting on the patio reading a book, when Grace arrived. "I got the last table. It's busy here tonight," she said. "I ordered you a glass of chardonnay and a margarita for me. I've already decided that I'm going to have lasagna."

Audrey loved Italian food. It didn't matter if it was the hottest day of the year, that's often what she ordered. And, Grace noted, Audrey didn't seem to think that a margarita and lasagna, were in the least incompatible. After a quick peruse of the menu, Grace ordered the salmon filet poached in white wine and herbs.

Grace and Audrey exchanged news of their respective days, with emphasis on the pressures at the probation department where there never seemed to be enough officers and interviews and reports were always more rushed than the officers would like. Grace didn't miss her days at Barnstable Probation. She was happy with her decision to buy Pearl's, but it was fun to talk with Audrey about their mutual friends and co-workers and catch up on the latest rumors floating around the courthouse.

Grace, who trusted Audrey explicitly and without reservation, filled her in on everything she knew about the assaults on Michael and Bella, as well as the break-in at Pearl's, which had left her sprawled on the hood of a car clinging to the windshield wipers, and then, of course, there was the mysterious dragonfly lamp.

"What's a dragonfly lamp?" Audrey asked.

"I'm not sure. The shape, the base, even the shade, could reference dragonflies. It could be a lot of things. I'm going to have to do some research and see what I can learn."

"Any thoughts about who might be looking for such a lamp?"

"At first I thought it might be some kind of deranged, confused collector," Grace said. But, now I don't think such a person would be so consistent in what they are looking for. But I am frightened. Whoever it is, they are desperate to find it and fast." Their entrees arrived, and she stared longingly at Audrey's lasagna.

"You always do this, Grace. Why not order the lasagna yourself?" she said, cutting off a piece and putting it on Grace's plate. After all, you're half Italian."

"The other half is Irish, and I'm in the mood for fish." Grace took another sip of her wine, savoring the buttery essence.

"I've made a new friend at the Asian Art history class I'm taking at the Community College," Audrey said. "I'm learning more about my ancestors every day. Anyway, her name is Julia Seymoor. I thought I'd ask her to join us on a run. She's from California, too."

"Is she married to Roone Seymoor?"

"Yes. How did you know?"

"He showed up at the murder scene the other day, shortly after we found Ben's body. And then I saw Roone and Julia at the wake, and today Roone came by Pearl's and purchased a Chinese jade lamp." Grace leaned forward in her chair. "Is that an odd coincidence, or am I imaging things?"

"I don't know, but the Cape is such a small place in many respects, that, coincidences as you know, often happen," Audrey observed, wiping her mouth, leaving a smear of pale lipstick on her napkin. "Julia's nice. She told me that she and Roone have been married for about five years. He's a successful entrepreneur in the tech field and travels a lot. They both love it here. She's taking a class in Asian Art history because eventually she wants to go into the antique appraising field. She decided to focus on Asian art, because Roone is apparently an avid collector of antiques and she wants to be able to share his interests, as well as having her own specialty. I think she said he's into twentieth century items."

'I'd like to meet her," Grace observed, curious about the woman she had seen at the wake, and wondered if she would be the recipient of the lamp Roone had purchased. And after a moment of hesitation, she decided to confide in Audrey.

"I think there might be something going on with Roone and a very attractive neighbor of theirs, named Luna," she said. "I saw them together at Ben's wake, and they were very chummy. Today, she followed him into Pearl's, and by the way she was touching him, and the way he responded, I have little doubt something is going on."

"Oh, I hope not!" Audrey exclaimed. "Julia seems to be very much in love with her husband, but she has been kind of on edge lately. I don't know her well enough to know if that is her personality. There does seem to be something unsettled about her. Maybe she senses that Roone's eye is more than wandering. "Oh. Weren't we just speaking of coincidences? Look who's here. It's Julia!"

Grace watched as the attractive woman, in khaki capris and a crisp white linen shirt approached them. Her dark hair framed her heart- shaped face beautifully. She had a warm smile for Audrey and greeted Grace with a formal handshake.

"I've been talking about you," Audrey said. "I wanted you two to meet because you've both lived in California."

"I lived in southern California," Julia said. "And you?"

"San Francisco."

"Very different places," Julia said "We should get together sometime and talk."

"Grace found the body of your neighbor, Ben Walwyn." Audrey announced.

"It's so distressing and shocking," she said, "It was such a short time ago that Imogene passed away, and now this horrible thing that happened to Ben. They were both such nice people."

"Did you know them well?" Grace asked, with what she hoped, sounded like normal curiosity. The truth was, she was far more interested in finding out who was searching for a valuable lamp, then anything to do with Ben's murder, but she had promised Bella, after all.

"Not really," Julia said, and then, after a pause, "when Imogene became ill, we started visiting more often. You know, in a neighborly kind of way. My husband, Roone, and I enjoyed Imogene's company. She was a delightful lady."

"And Ben?"

"Between us women - now please don't laugh at me - but I thought he was kind of sexy, in a rough kind of way. Do you think I'm crazy?"

Audrey burst out laughing. "No, not crazy. You could tell that he was once a really handsome man, and he did have some charm - when sober, that is."

"I know what you both are alluding to," Grace said, amused by the conversation, yet at the same time realizing that they were venturing into unseemly territory, given Ben's recent passing. "I wonder exactly what it is that often attracts women to the bad boys," she added.

"Maybe they're bad girls," Julia said, in such a way that Grace felt that she had strong feelings about the subject. She recalled Julia, at Ben's service, blocking Freesia's way into the viewing area.

"Well, it's sad that he didn't stay charming, and sober," Grace added.

"And alive," added Audrey.

The three nodded in agreement, the way women sometimes do, when something is obvious, and there is nothing more to say.

Chapter Twenty- Seven

Grace had only been home only a few minutes, when she saw headlights in her driveway. Could Felix have rented a car? Now that would be a surprise, she thought, as, answering a knock on her kitchen door, she saw Andre and Frank, his German Shepherd. Although responsive to Andre's commands, Frank, one scary looking dog, had flunked out of police canine training.

Grace bent down to rub his head. Frank leaned against her with what appeared to her to be a smile on his face.

"Frank! So wonderful to see you," Grace said. It was true. She had grown very fond of Andre's dogs, Frank and Lola.

"Wonderful to see me, too?" Andre asked, looking hopeful.

With some difficulty, Grace held back a smile. "What brings you here tonight?"

"Had some thoughts to run by you, he said and taking a deep breath, plunged into the conversation as though it hadn't been a dozen or more hours since they last spoke. "Someone is looking for a lamp. For whatever reason, they think that this lamp is at Pearl's, or that someone there knows something about it. Is it possible that you have a lamp that is more valuable than you might ordinarily have? Anyone bring in something expensive for repairs? "

"We do have some very nice lamps, but I don't think we have anything that would make someone go to these lengths to get their hands on it," Grace told him. "Bella and Michael keep a close eye on the inventory because the antique business is so susceptible to frauds and fakes. Anything could slip by me, of course, but Bella would spot something of real value. She has years of experience and knows how to check for clarity, type of glass, seams, and even the way in which a base might have been attached. She's an expert and has established a reputation as a knowledgeable appraiser in the lamp world."

"There's a lamp world?" Andre chuckled. "Who knew?"

Ignoring Andre's amusement, she continued. "Pearl's has been in a lot of turmoil these past couple of weeks because of the move. Duane's been moving boxes all over the place, from Beau's, to here, and to Michael's. It's possible something new could have slipped in for a repair but I doubt it."

Andre nodded. "I spoke with Sophie, the little girl who hangs around the village," Andre said. "She saw a man with boots. He was wearing a dark blue sweatshirt."

"Not much to go on."

"No, and an antique shop in Centerville was burglarized last night. The owners are taking inventory to determine what might have been stolen. I might think this was someone looking in all of the antique shops on Cape Cod for a particular lamp, maybe a stolen lamp, but for one thing."

"Bella?"

"Yes. Michael was in the shop, so it's not a surprise that he was attacked, but Bella was attacked in her home. When Bella couldn't or wouldn't tell them what they wanted to know, they moved on to other shops. But, I doubt they have given up, and I think Bella is in extreme danger."

"Couldn't or wouldn't tell them? What on earth do you mean?"

"Bella has been cooperative with the officers' inquiry, but because of her age, and the circumstances, they are reluctant to push her too hard. I'm thinking that maybe, when she's up to it, you might talk to her and see if there is anything we've overlooked, or if there is anything she might have forgotten."

"You're asking me to help in the investigation?" Grace's eyes opened wide. This was a new development. Andre had been very unhappy when she inserted herself into last year's murder investigation.

Andre gave her a long stare, not the Andre stare that she had at one time grown to love, but the stare that meant he wasn't happy with the way the conversation was going.

"I'm leaving Frank with you," he said. "Unless you think your houseguest will protect you."

"He's often away, but I'm quite sure he would come to my rescue if the occasion should arise. He seems more than capable."

"Take my advice and send him home."

"I'm enjoying his company. He's a big help around here. Why should I take your advice on this?"

"Because I'm trying my best to keep all of you safe," Andre said angrily. "You're taking a risk having him around when so many bad things are happening."

In the back of her mind, Grace realized she might have been taking her efforts to make Andre jealous too far, but she remained silent.

Andre glared at her. "I'm going to leave Frank here anyway."

"But what about Clambake?"

"Didn't you tell me that Clambake could hold his own with dogs?"

Grace recalled one of her first encounters with Andre. "I guess I did say that."

"Okay, well then, he's all yours. Here's his food and instructions." With that he handed Grace Frank's leash and left without another word.

.

Chapter Twenty- Eight

White cotton curtains fluttered over Grace's kitchen sink, and the breeze ruffled her hair as she cleaned up yet another of Felix's messes. Last evening, after Andre left, she'd taken a shower, climbed into bed, and slept like a baby, too tired to be fearful of any knocks or bumps that might have occurred during the night. But this morning it was all too clear that Felix must have made himself a late snack. An empty ice cream carton lay on its side in the sink, mustard and mayonnaise jars were on the table, and a loaf of bread had not been sealed, inviting moisture, which left an icky green mold on the remaining two pieces, which she promptly tossed in the garbage. In fact, wasn't that an ant climbing over a slice of deli turkey half hidden by a dirty napkin?

Ugh! She'd kill him. That was the only possible solution, she thought. Clearly she had suffered some sort of decline in her mental abilities when, a few nights ago, she had considered that Felix might possess some redeeming qualities. After all, anyone would have called 911 under the circumstances. She sighed. Only a short time left and Felix would just be a bad memory. Surely, the day might come when she might even laugh about the crazy week she'd spent with Felix. That day couldn't come too soon.

Letting Frank in from his brief sniff around the back patio, she filled his bowl and gave him a biscuit. Clambake, who clearly was unhappy about this large canine interloper, was sitting on top of Grace's worktable amidst her papers and shade supplies. Last night had gone reasonably well, with Clambake in her bed, as usual, and Frank on a makeshift bed of old blankets, in her bedroom doorway, and with any luck, Frank, like Felix, would be heading home soon.

As Grace wiped crumbs off the table, she noticed Felix's notebook. Curious, she lifted the cover and flipped through several pages of notes. Earlier, when she came downstairs, she'd heard heavy snoring coming from her guestroom, so a bit of snooping was safe enough. Besides, she told herself, it was never too late to find out more about her houseguest. She couldn't imagine what kind of writer he could be. A journalist? Not likely.

On top of the first page, Felix had written in a surprisingly neat script, 'Characters, how to create,' on top of one page and 'Denouement' on another. Several folded handouts were stuffed in between pages. There were plenty of doodles of naked women, too. She shook her head. Hopeless, he was hopeless. She flipped some more pages and found a section titled 'Pearl's;' followed by a list of items found in the shop, including lamps, shades, tools, and cash register, as well as a map of the store layout in detail, noting the location of the doors and windows. It was lightly sketched, but pretty darned accurate, considering he had only spent a short time in the shop. Perhaps he was a quick study after all.

She closed the notebook when she heard Felix's heavy tread on her bare wood stairs. "Hey, Felix," she greeted him.

"Hey, yourself," he replied, throwing a pair of dirty sandals on the floor and easing his large feet into them. "I can't stop and chat with you. I'm late for class." The screen door closed sharply behind him.

Grace declined to add rude to the long list of personality defects that immediately came to her mind. On the other hand, he was gone. And gone was good.

When she ran upstairs to get dressed for work, she found the guest room door open. Felix always closed it, but today, in his rush he must have forgotten. She drifted in. After all, it *was* her guest room. The bed was unmade, and papers and candy wrappers littered the floor. To think that she had worried about cleaning the house before he arrived, she thought.

Because the closet door was ajar as well, she sidled over to it and was faced with what seemed a score of blue jeans, shorts, and tee shirts. The light blanket, that, as a rule, was kept on the guest bed for the occasional chilly night was balled up on the floor. She picked it up and shook it out. Underneath was a laptop.

Sitting on the bed, she opened the lid, and was contemplating her next move, when she heard the back door slam and heard Felix's heavy tread on the stairs. He was moving fast, and within seconds he entered the room, giving her just enough time to return the blanket and laptop to the closet.

To say he was surprised to find her there would be an understatement, judging by the look of irritation on his face.

"You looking for something?" he demanded.

"No. I mean, yes," Grace stammered. "I couldn't find Clambake. Your door was open, and I thought he might be in here. Cats are so curious."

"He's on the couch in the living room. I passed him on the way up here."

"Oh .That's good to know. I was afraid he might have gotten outside again."

Felix went to the closet, picked up his laptop, and left the house.

But not before giving her a look of barely concealed contempt.

Chapter Twenty-Nine

Although Pearl's was not officially re-opened, Grace had taken down the closed sign, allowing locals to meander through, have coffee, and even conduct a bit of lamp business. Any formal opening would have to be delayed until the mysteries that had brought fear, uncertainty and anger were resolved. A man stopped by to drop off a brass lamp for repair. Another customer picked out a large black empire shade for a striking silver lamp in the shape of a lobster. She seemed pleased with the shade that Grace had helped her to select, and Grace was relieved because she didn't have the expertise that Michael did when it came to choosing the right shade for a lamp. The height and width of the lamp had to be taken into consideration, the purpose of the lamp and the overall design. Furthermore, the best color choice wasn't always obvious to her. Michael knew what questions to ask the shopper, and always picked out the perfect shade.

Setting out a pair of glass cylinder lamps, Grace admired the tiny glass beads that had been affixed to the etched flower design by enamel, a process known as coralene. Giving the pull chains a tug, she turned them on and marveled at the glow from the lamps, reflected in the mirror that she and Duane had hung over the mantle of a now closed up fireplace.

"These are so nice," she said.

"Guess so," Duane, said, shoving a piece of salt water taffy in his mouth, and chewing furiously. "I'm going through our inventory and checking twice, as you said I should, to see if anything is missing. I've got everything that was stored with Michael. I'll check upstairs with Beau and make triple sure that we're good to go. Don't want to forget anything," he added, emphasizing the words 'missing' and 'forget.' "Then, I'll go by your house and let Frank out for a spell, and after that, make a quick run to Emma's house to check on her canary, Petey."

Duane frequently made trips to see the bird, and Grace figured, as she heard the thud of feet as he climbed the outside stairs to the bookshop, he was trying hard to be conscientious in his house and pet sitting duties. All in all, Duane was working out fine. She had to remind him of things and put up with the flaws in his "system," but he was wiry and strong, and that was sorely needed around Pearl's.

Seeing a movement on the porch, she looked out the window to see Owen Walwyn peering in, after which he proceeded to enter the shop and saunter up to her worktable, with what she took to be a strange mix of self-consciousness and bravado.

"Bella here?" he grunted.

"No, she's not here right now. Can I help you with something?"

"I need to reach her. Give me her phone number."

"I'm sorry. I can't give that information out," Grace answered.

"She's a friend of the family, and I need to talk to her."

"That may be, but I still can't give you her number."

As Grace looked into his eyes, Ben's face flashed uncomfortably through her memory. Ben's eyes, of course, had not been clear on the day she met him, but they had the same deep-sea intensity that she was staring at right now.

"I know where she lives," he asserted. "I went by there this morning."

Grace didn't respond, waiting for Owen to reveal something more. Could he have attacked Bella? After all, what did anyone know about him? Nothing, as far as she knew.

"Maybe I'll just hang out here until she comes in," he said, placing both hands on her counter in an intimidating way.

Grace's impression of the young man was going from bad to worse. One thing for sure, she was not going to let him try to bully her.

"Give me your name and number, and when I see Bella, I'll give it to her," she said. "If she wants to contact you, she will. If you're shopping for a lamp or shade, feel free to look around. Otherwise, I don't let people just hang out in the shop."

Owen scowled but took a piece of her drawing paper and scrawled his first name, and a number. "Don't forget to give it to her, or I will be back, and I will hang out until I see her," he warned.

"Fat chance," Grace said, as he turned away with an air of nonchalance that she doubted was sincere. At the door, he gave her the one finger salute.

The same salute she had witnessed, his father, Ben, serve notice to Mason Crawford, on the day that he died.

Chapter Thirty

"**W**e're back!" Bella said, bursting through the door. "And raring to go."

"I've brought in my espresso machine," Michael announced proudly, looking dapper in a cream colored linen suit that was probably decades old, but of a timeless style, which he had complimented with a black and white striped bow tie. "My goodness. This looks so lovely. What a difference a day or so makes around here. I can't wait to start setting up the Aladdin Beehive lamps. They will look gorgeous in the window, especially in the afternoon when the sun will pour in and the jewel colors will positively glow." And with that, he trundled off in the direction of the kitchen, saying, "I'll make some coffee, and it will be like the old Pearl's. I hope you all have your coffee cups."

Grace watched Bella toss a pair of gray tweed slippers on the floor and step into them, leaving about two inches of heel hanging over the tweedy soles.

"I can't believe you're here," Grace exclaimed. "Shouldn't you both be resting?"

"I'll rest when I'm dead," Bella replied. "Michael was kind enough to lend me a pair of his slippers. My goodness, that man has tiny feet."

"Oh Bella, you might as well go barefoot," Grace said.

"I could, I suppose, but I have a pair of sneakers back here somewhere," she said, as she rummaged around in her workstation. "I sure have a lot of sorting to do before I can start catching up on lamp repairs."

"Ben's son, Owen, came by today," Grace told her. "He said he wants to talk to you. I wouldn't give him your number, but here's his if you want to contact him."

"Oh, yes, I do. Thank you."

Grace was disturbed by Bella's readiness to get in touch with Owen. "Do you think it's a good idea to call him? We don't know anything about him. In fact, we don't even know if he is Ben's son."

"Did you get a look at him? He's the image of Ben. Couldn't be anyone else's son."

"That may be true, but we don't know anything about what kind of person he is," Grace said, unwilling to give up.

"I think I'm a good judge of character," Bella assured her. "In any case, I'm going to call him. And, taking your point into consideration, I won't meet with him alone."

Now, apparently because Michael was clattering dishes in the kitchen area and thus safely out of hearing, Bella said, "I *had* to come to work today. Michael has been driving me nuts. He's so neat and tidy, always cleaning this and straightening up that. He's so used to living alone, his equilibrium has been disturbed, poor man." Bella said. "Did you know that he has never left Cape Cod? Never even been to Boston,"

"Yes, he told me," Grace said. "He has no interest in travel and is perfectly content at home."

"Until I arrived," Bella chuckled.

✳✳✳✳✳

Grace found Michael in the kitchen, scowling at the refrigerator. "I've only been gone a day and look what a mess this is!" he exclaimed, gathering cleaning supplies.

"Surely, Michael, you're exaggerating," Grace said, but added, "Of course, things are not the same when you're away. I'm worried about you. Are you sure you feel all right?"

"That man didn't hurt us," Michael said, with strength in his voice that Grace had never heard before. "Bella and I are a couple of tough old goats. And besides, we'll never let anyone scare us from our work and our friends. Don't worry, Grace, we're safe as can be. Remember," he went on, wiping crumbs from a shelf, "Andre is staying with us. He's teaching us to play pedro, that's a card game, and he's a whiz at Scrabble. By the way, have you ever tasted his Portuguese stew? Amazing."

She nodded, remembering last winter when Andre had invited her to his house for dinner. He was a gifted cook, a skill for which she had no interest or talent.

Bella appeared in the kitchen, slowly moving her tall frame in the direction of a chair by the window. "Andre is such a dear. Made us a breakfast of blueberry pancakes," she said, and then added with a thoughtful look, "I hesitate to speak out of turn, but I do believe he is still very interested in you."

Grace frowned. Andre knew blueberry pancakes were her favorites, and yet, he hadn't offered to make her any when he slept on her couch. All she got was one sip of his bitter black coffee.

Games, cards, Portuguese stew, and blueberry pancakes for breakfast. It was obvious the three of them were having a pretty good time at Michael's. And, what did she have? Felix and Frank. That's what.

"Grace, I need to talk to you about something that's been on my mind," Bella said, changing the subject after apparently recognizing Grace's reluctance to comment on her observations regarding Andre. "I discussed it with Michael this morning, and he agreed I should tell you. Do you have your notebook handy?"

After pouring Bella a cup of coffee, Michael, placing it on a yellow embroidered napkin that he knew she favored, slid a pad of paper and a pen across the table in Grace's direction.

"It's about this lamp that someone is looking for," Bella said, clearing her throat. "A valuable lamp that Imogene had for a long time. Actually, Imogene stole it."

"Stole it?" Grace asked. "What do you mean?"

Bella gazed at the ceiling and sighed deeply. "I feel terrible having to tell anyone about this, even those I trust explicitly. I loved Imogene and I promised her I would never tell. But, if we're going to get to the bottom of Ben's murder and all the rest of the strange things going on around here, I know I have to do it." Bella took off her glasses and rubbed her eyes. "I guess the best way is to say it like it is. Imogene had a bit of a problem. She liked pretty things. She would often 'borrow' them, as she used to call it. During the years I returned many a borrowed item to its rightful owner. As far as I know, no one ever figured out that Imogene was involved. She couldn't seem to help herself. And, I must admit, I think she rather enjoyed the excitement."

"Did she ask you to return these items for her?"

"No, I just did it on my own. I'd make up an excuse of some sort, or leave the item on a front porch, or package it, and drop it in the mail. I didn't want her to get in trouble. I sometimes think it was all a game to her," she sighed. "I tried to get her to seek professional help, but, as far as I know, she never consulted anyone. As time went on, she got bolder and managed to take some very expensive things. One day, shortly before she departed this earth, when she was more or less bedridden, I was visiting with her and I noticed a striking lamp on her bedside table. I asked her about it, and she admitted that she had 'borrowed' it from an antique lamp shop in Boston more than fifty years ago. This type of lamp wasn't as popular or valuable as they are now. In fact, there was a time when folks threw them out or donated them to thrift stores. Very few collectors were interested in them. Not that that excuses what she did," Bella added. "She said she would leave it up to me to decide what to do about it. I didn't want this burden, but she was so ill."

That was so like Bella, Grace thought, always thinking of others.

"When she died, I tried my best to get the children together," Bella continued. "The rightful owner had to be located, but there were bad feelings after Imogene's will was read. When Ben came to see me, on his last day on this earth, he told me that Imogene had told them about it shortly before she died. She didn't tell them everything of course. She told them the value of the lamp, but not that it was stolen. I didn't say anything to Ben about the provenance of the lamp. Instead I asked him to arrange a time with William and Portia when I could meet with all of them. There was something about the lamp that I needed to tell them right away."

Bella was, Grace observed, more troubled than she'd ever

seen her.

"Ben said the lamp was his, he'd inherited all of the property in the house. He could use the money from selling it, but for now, he planned to keep it," Bella explained. "He didn't want to meet with William and Portia. I wasn't sure what to do, and before I could do anything, Ben was dead, and the lamp wasn't by Imogene's bedside anymore. And, then Michael and I were attacked and...I've been so confused."

Grace put her hand on Bella's shoulder. "Do you think besides William and Portia, anyone else might know about the lamp and its value?"

"I don't know. But, once her children knew about it, who knows? William probably told Morgan, and Portia would have told Trevor, and Ben may have told his friend Freesia. And from there...?" Bella wrung her hands.

"How valuable is this lamp?"

"As I mentioned, when Imogene "borrowed" it, the style had gone out of favor. But now..."

"Now? What kind of style?" Grace asked, not being able to wait a second more.

"It's a Tiffany. Louis Comfort Tiffany, that is. In a dragonfly design. And despite trouble with its shaky provenance, it's worth hundreds of thousands of dollars. And, like anything of value, there's a flourishing black market."

Grace gasped. "Are you serious? A Tiffany Dragonfly? Is it original?" she asked, knowing the vast number of reproductions and out right fakes that were always on the market.

Bella nodded, her hands now quiet on her lap.

The bell on the front door of the shop chimed and a few seconds later, Andre appeared in the doorway of the little kitchen. Nodding at Michael and Bella, and ignoring Grace in what she took to be lingering anger over their recent argument about Felix, he said. "When I saw the front of the shop was empty, I was worried." He sniffed the air, fragrant with roasting coffee beans. "Michael must be back in business with his espresso machine. Is there any left?" He leaned against the counter. "Why are you all so quiet?"

Michael pushed back his chair and padded over to the espresso machine. Grace looked expectantly at Bella who nodded and said, "Of course. We must tell Andre. I feel terrible. Bad things are happening to those I love."

Pulling out a handkerchief she blew her nose, and then, proceeded to tell Andre about the rare lamp.

"I didn't know a lamp could be worth so much," Andre said. "Now, I see why someone wants to get their hands on it."

"Oh yes," Michael piped up, "The most expensive lamp that I've heard about, is a Tiffany Lotus. It sold a while back for almost three million dollars. Many more of them are in the hundreds of thousand-dollar range. It depends on the style, rarity, and condition, of course."

"Okay, so, Ben, William, and Portia knew about the existence and the value of the lamp, but not that Imogene had stolen it," Andre said. "Imogene may have told others, and Ben might have told some of his many untrustworthy friends. Bella might have solved one mystery. I would bet that there's more than a good chance that Ben was murdered for this lamp."

"Yes, I'm afraid so," Bella cried. "And, for some reason, they think I have it. But, I don't have any idea where it is."

They all jumped when the front bell jangled again, and footsteps thundered down the hallway. Andre moved to the door.

"I'm in big trouble," Duane said, breathlessly as he burst into the room.

"What's happened?" Andre asked him.

"I was cleaning up Emma's house," Duane said, clearly distraught. "It wasn't really dirty, but I was hoping I would impress her, and she'd ask me to house sit again sometime."

"Duane, just get to the point," Andre demanded.

"I let Petey out of his cage for some exercise. Then, I dusted and vacuumed. I opened some windows for fresh air. Duane gulped. "And Petey flew away!"

"Oh Duane," Grace said, trying to digest this latest news. How was it that he managed to find himself in the most preposterous circumstances?

"When does Emma get back from Boston?" Duane asked Andre.

"Tonight."

"She is going to kill me!"

"You're right about that," Andre said.

Bella and Michael looked at each other with surprise. "Who's Petey?" they asked at once.

Grace stifled a smile. A canary and a valuable Tiffany lamp were missing. Could the day have become any stranger?

*****

When Grace went to lock up the shop, she found Michael and Bella on the front porch.

"What a beautiful evening," Michael exclaimed. "Everything looks rosy, and the air is sweet."

Labor Day had come and gone, taking many of the Cape's summer visitors home to their real lives, over the bridges, to Connecticut, New Hampshire, and Vermont. The days were temperate, and fall, Grace's favorite season, would be here soon.

Main Street was calm, most of the businesses having closed a few hours ago. Even the old courthouse on the hill was quiet, with only a few lawyers, probation officers, and defendants still milling around.

A red sedan pulled up, and an arm wrapped in gold bracelets waved from the driver's window. "Hi Bella, do you have a minute?" the woman called out.

"Hi, Luna," Bella replied. "What can I do for you?"

"I'm doing some errands and thought I'd stop by and see how you're doing. What a terrible thing to happen to you."

When Bella introduced Michael and Grace, Luna nodded at them in a disinterested way. Neither Luna nor Grace mentioned her earlier visit to Pearl's.

"Can I talk to you in private, Bella?"she asked.

Grace and Michael excused themselves and sat a polite distance away on the bench under planter boxes filled with scraggly flowers and weeds. Tomorrow, Grace thought, she would plant something anything, in those boxes. Rising, she proceeded to pull out the dead plants as Michael seized the opportunity to tell Grace what it was like to have Bella as his houseguest, how she was a tad messy and so on. Grace didn't want to be rude, and she certainly didn't want to be caught between her two employees, but what she really wanted to do was clap her hand over his mouth, so she could hear what Luna had to say, and to that end moved to the edge of the porch, closer to the two women. Michael, not one to be ignored, continued with his list of complaints, which included such crimes as Bella's leaving a jar of jam on the table, rather than immediately returning it to the fridge.

"Oh, and she left the hall light on too, although she was the last to go to bed," he added as Luna drove off leaving Grace none the wiser about why she had come by.

"That's interesting," Bella said, joining them, "Luna said she saw me on the porch and decided she might as well stop and ask me if Ben had mentioned anything about some personal items that Imogene may have set aside for her. She said that Imogene told her that she could have some antique items, including a table, a couple of crystal vases and a lamp. She said that she was hoping I might be aware of Imogene's desire for Luna to be the recipient of these sentimental but valueless articles. She planned to talk to William or Portia in time, but she didn't want to be unsympathetic to their grief. It seems that word about the Tiffany may have traveled further than we thought. "My goodness, why does everyone seem to think that I know something?"

"Because you were Imogene's best friend, and you know everything about lamps," Michael volunteered.

Grace was thoughtful for a minute. "You might not know anything Bella, but maybe you *have* something." Grace said. "Didn't you say that Ben had dropped some personal items off here on the day he was murdered?"

"Yes, a box of what I suppose, are old photographs and letters, that sort of thing. I haven't had a chance to go through everything. I assume its sentimental items. It was thoughtful of Ben to bring them to me."

"Where's the box now?" Grace asked with growing excitement.

"I haven't a clue, now that you mention it. I think I left it on the back step where we were smoking. But, that was several days ago. I'm sorry Grace; I'm so tired, I can't think straight." Taking Michael's arm, she said, "Let's go back to your house and have a cocktail and a nap before dinner. How does chicken and dumplings sound to you?"

The two friends began to walk down the street. Bella stopped and turned around. "We'll have to ask Duane," she told Grace. "He's in charge of boxes."

Grace groaned, to think that Duane and his confused 'system' of moving boxes around might hold the key to the whereabouts of a very valuable missing Tiffany lamp. She reached for her cell. Duane had gone back to Emma's, too distraught to work, for another search for Petey. When he answered her call, she asked him about the box that Ben had brought for Bella.

"Ms. Tolliver. I don't know anything about a box that Bella got from Ben. I moved all of the boxes that were around the shop, to Michael's house and to your barn. I've brought everything back to the shop." He paused. "Am I in trouble?"

"No Duane." At least not with me, she thought, thinking of Emma and the now lost Petey. "Besides putting boxes in storage, did you do any deliveries of repaired lamps lately?"

"Yup, one. I wrote it down in the logbook, like I'm supposed to."

After assuring Duane a few more times, that he wasn't in trouble and ending the call, Grace scanned her records. Duane had made a delivery of a repaired lamp and a new shade to Mr. Jake Stonely, a customer in Hyannis Port, the day that Ben came to the shop. It was certainly possible that Duane might have picked up Bella's boxes, where she had left them on the back porch, and delivered them in error to her customer. It was, she knew a long shot, but one worth investigating.

Chapter Thirty- One

Grace was planning on driving over to Cotuit to check on her dad and Gink. If she had time, she'd stop off at Mr. Stonely's on her way home. She was leaving the store, her car keys in hand and a bag of groceries for her dad, when Clay hurried up the front steps.

"Grace, this is Tia Jones," Clay said, indicating a slim woman, with large black sunglasses. "From New York City," Clay said. When Grace must have looked perplexed, he added, "From the inn, about those shades I told you about."

"Oh! Please come in."

Grace backed into the shop and extended her hand to the woman who was busy adjusting her black and white polka dotted scarf that was wrapped, just so, around her thin neck. She took Grace's hand for a fraction of a second and peered at her over half-moon spectacles as if she were examining a portrait in a museum and not a flesh and blood person standing two feet in front of her. Her perfectly proportioned dress and very high heels were black. She certainly looked stunning, but as out of place on Cape Cod on a September afternoon as a fisherman in waders would be on Park Avenue.

Tia marched quickly around the shop, said, "Charming," and then got down to business, wasting no time describing what she wanted in the way of shades for the refurbished inn and when the order would have to be completed. She then went to some length to describe her idea of whenever possible, searching out and engaging, locally sourced goods for her decorating project.

"After all, our guests will appreciate local crafts," she

declared. "A 'win-win' for all involved."

Grace remembered Clay's fondness for the same irritating and overused phrase, but despite the cliché, it was a nice sounding plan indeed.

Without further ado, Tia said that she needed thirty shades. Half were to be made of plain white linen, the other half to be hand painted. She would leave the individual designs to Grace, but she wanted a beach and sand dune Cape Cod type of theme. Each shade should be unique and feature only four colors; blue, green, fawn and peach. Various shades and hues of these colors were permissible as long as Grace stuck to her guidelines. In conclusion, she handed Grace a paper detailing the sizes of the shades. On the bottom of the page was a dollar amount. It was a sizeable number.

"We're prepared to pay to get the quality that we desire," Tia said. "Is that figure acceptable to you?"

"Yes, quite acceptable," Grace said, holding back an excited stammer. It was more than acceptable and was a generous sum. But, her elation subsided when Tia said, "I must have them in two weeks. Delivered and no excuses for delay."

Grace hesitated, as she looked down at the figures on the paper her hand shaking either from nerves, or excitement, or both. Tia was clearly a woman in a hurry and Grace knew the old saying, time is money, applied to this job. But, could she deliver? The shop was behind on orders due to construction. The events of the past week had been exhausting and overwhelming for all. Bella would certainly add that they were investigating a murder, as well.

"What do you think?" Tia asked. "I really need an answer now. If it's not something you can commit to, I'll go elsewhere. I hope we can reach an agreement. I've heard so much about your product."

Grace had never imagined her handmade shades as "product." Such a silly and vague sounding word, she thought. They were, after all, special, distinctive, and inspired. They were works of art, all of them.

"Have you decided?" Tia asked impatiently.

Her attention having been brought back sharply to the decision at hand, Grace took one quick glance at the estimate. It was a great opportunity to get her shades in this beautiful inn where visitors to the Cape could see her shades someplace other than her small shop.

"Yes, I can do this." Grace heard what sounded like her own voice, confidently making a promise to Tia, a promise that, at this moment, seemed impossible.

"Good, we're in agreement. I've got the paperwork right here," Tia said, unzipping an elegant briefcase. "Thank you, Grace. I'm really pleased that we will be doing business. I'm sincere about promoting locals. You see, I'm originally from Cape Cod."

"No kidding," Grace said, totally surprised by this revelation. There had been nothing about Tia, as far as she could see, that suggested Cape Cod.

"I knew the Walwyn family," Tia continued. "Clay told me you found Ben's body. I went to school with Portia. I even dated William a couple of times."

"Oh," was all Grace managed to say.

"William was quite a nice person," Tia went on. "Not my type though. But Portia was another story. I heard she married well, which is a good thing, because she had what might be called delusions of grandeur. All she talked about was the price of this and the price of that. At the same time, she didn't have any ambitions of her own. She acted like she was entitled to the finer things in life without having to earn them herself."

"Sounds like she was spoiled."

"I think Imogene spoiled all of her children. Their father died when they were young. They never seemed to have any money worries though." Tia glanced at her watch. "Oh my goodness, it's later than I thought. I'll be talking to you soon. Clay, I need coffee asap."

Clay, heaving a sigh, apparently relieved he put this deal together, and probably imaging more commissions from Tia, nodded heartily. "Nirvana. Right across the street."

As for Grace, reeling from her promise to Tia and all the

other troubling things on her mind, realized that a touch of nirvana, and not necessarily the caffeine kind, might well serve her, too.

Chapter Thirty-Two

Grace climbed into her 1948 Ford panel truck, which was emblazoned with Pearl's logo, pictures of lamps and shades, personified with happy smiles. Some of the shades even had legs and appeared to be dancing. Truth was, she hated the logo left over from Matt and Milo's days. She had planned to have the truck painted with something more to her taste. Somehow, with all that needed to be done around the shop, it hadn't happened yet.

Heading south to Cotuit where her father lived, she became nervous as she thought about the commitment she'd made to Tia. Fifteen minutes was all it had taken for her to agree to do the impossible. Now, although she was excited about the job, she was anxious, too. At the best of times, getting this done in two weeks would be a tall order. And this was far from the best of times.

As Grace maneuvered her truck into her dad's narrow lane, she came upon Thomas DePaci weaving down the road on his bicycle. Wearing rubber flip-flops and baggy shorts, his white hair was wind-blown, giving him the look of a wayward tourist. A blue towel was wrapped around his neck and he was singing, "My Way." When she followed him into his driveway, he immediately stopped his bike, and reached in the wicker basket for his helmet, and stuck it on his head.

"Dad, I thought we agreed that you'd wear your helmet," she protested. "If you fall, you could really hurt yourself." Grace wasn't entirely happy with her dad riding his bike to the beach. It wasn't far, and the exercise was good for him, but since she worried about him falling, they had compromised in regard to the helmet.

"I am wearing it," Thomas said.

"I just saw you put it on."

"No, you didn't."

Grace remembered her vow that she would not try to fix what couldn't be fixed, and to that end, murmured the words, "Don't go there," several times under her breath. It was part of her new weapon against frustration and possible insanity.

"Okay, Dad. Whatever," she said, assuming a cheerfulness that was far from what she was feeling.

"What are you doing here? Are you staying for supper? There's leftover meatloaf."

"No, I just dropped by to see how you are."

"Well, Gracie, as you can see, I'm just fine. I had a wonderful swim in the bay. The water temp was near perfect. Next time, you might want to come with me."

"Good idea," she said.

Entering the back yard, Grace was startled to see a portable wooden fence surrounding an irregular patch of grass.

"What's that for?" she asked.

"The sheep," her father replied, as if that were the most rational thing in the world.

"Sheep? What are you talking about?" Grace said, as a small furry white creature darted from behind a maple tree followed by another, roughly the same size. "Oh my God!"

"Cute, aren't they?"

They *were* cute. Possibly the cutest animals Grace had ever seen. When she walked over to the pen, the sheep ran to her. Reaching down, she petted their soft wooly heads.

"But what are they doing here?" Grace asked, half afraid to hear her father's reply.

"Look what a great job they're doing on the grass," he told her. "I have an idea for a unique business. I'm going to rent them out as lawn mowers."

Repeating her mantra to herself, once again, Grace went into her father's kitchen and placed the groceries on the table.

"Where's Gink?" she asked. "What does she think of the new additions to your household?"

"I think she's sleeping. She was when I left."

"Is she sick?"

"I don't think so. Tired, I guess."

"Well, then, why don't you ride with me to Hyannis Port?" Grace said, noting the absence of any dinner preparation. I need to run a quick errand. It shouldn't take long and we can stop at Monti's Clam Shack on the way. It doesn't look like Gink has started dinner. I'll leave her a note."

As soon as he'd changed into khakis and a green shirt adorned with sailboats, they settled themselves on the worn seats of her truck, and rolled down their windows, letting the salty warm breeze tousle their hair as they set out for the shore. There was a comfortable silence between them as they drove into the summer evening's golden hue. Despite their occasional disagreements, usually caused by one worrying too much about the other, they had a way of being together that was easy and comfortable.

*****

Thomas was clearly happy as he slid into a chair by the window at Monti's, his favorite café. The clams were good, the view of the harbor at sunset gorgeous, and her dad was pleased that he had a chance to visit with his favorite waitress. Later, in the darkening evening they drove the short distance to her customer, Mr. Stonley's house in Hyannis Port. Grace pulled up in front of a shingled, two-story house located a few blocks from where the Kennedy compound was located, which sported a wide veranda and a pair of white rocking chairs to greet visitors. The front porch light was on.

"I'll wait here," Thomas said.

"Okay. This should just take a minute."

Vaguely aware that a car had turned up the road, headlights briefly lighting up the yard of a neighboring house as it parked at the curb, Grace ran up the stairs, hoping this visit would be quick, and she could hurry home, to her sure to be starving

Clambake.

The front door was opened by a genial appearing man who looked quizzically at Grace as she introduced herself and explained to him about the possible mix up. Had he had a chance to open the boxes that Duane had delivered?

"Indeed I did," he told her. "I love what Bella did with my lamp. All shiny and clean and working great. Would you care to see it? It's right here in my study."

Grace didn't want to linger, particularly since she had found out what she needed to know. The Tiffany lamp was not here. Not wanting to be rude, however, she followed her customer through a living room and into his study, where a very nice antique desk lamp with a classic green shade stood gleaming on a cherry wood desk. Grace recognized the lamp at once. She had admired it when Bella was polishing it.

"I'm so happy with it," the man said, leading the way back to the foyer. "May I give you another lamp to clean up? A new shade is needed too, and Bella could see if it needs new wires. It's been blinking on and off. I don't want to start a fire. It would save me a trip. I'll put it in the box your employee delivered."

After Grace discussed various lampshade possibilities with him, which included drum, square, round empire, even hexagonal, he appeared, overwhelmed by the possibilities. He said he would trust her judgment. She took the lamp and bid the man goodnight.

Glancing in the window of her truck and seeing that her dad was asleep, Grace popped open the back door and carefully placed Mr. Stonely's lamp inside. Since her customer had not received the wrong package, the best thing to do, she thought, would be to get together with Bella and take a look through her cluttered house for the missing boxes. Of course, it wasn't clear that Bella even had the lamp. The only thing that *was* clear was that someone thought she did. And, to be safe, she'd ask Duane to go through her barn again and have Michael double check his house for the missing box.

Suddenly, someone wearing a hooded sweatshirt shoved her roughly to the ground, and before she could get up, they grabbed the box and started running down the block. By the time Grace was on her feet that someone jumped into a vehicle and took off with a screech of tires.

*****

Thomas, having slept through the incident in Hyannis port, was berating himself for being useless, and not helping Grace.

"I'm glad you were asleep," she assured him. "There's nothing you could have done, Dad."

"I could have seen him coming, got a good description and chased him down."

Grace contemplated her dad's comment. Possibly the first two were true, but the last was doubtful. "Don't worry. Nobody was hurt," she said, kissing him on his cheek. And then, noticing that the house was quiet and that there was no sign of Gink. "Do you think she's still sleeping? When did you last see her?"

"She went to bed around four," he told her.

"I wonder if she's all right," Grace said, alarmed that Gink might be so ill that she was still in bed. Her father, however, simply shrugged and turned on the TV.

"I'm going to go upstairs and check on her," she said.

Gink was sprawled on the bed, breathing heavily, when Grace touched her lightly on the arm. Gink muttered something, which sounded like "Uh oh."

It was then that Grace noticed the tall glass, and the bottle of gin on the nightstand.

Chapter Thirty-Three

Andre was on the patio where Grace had sent him to calm down after she had told him about her latest incident in Hyannis Port. He was savoring the last drop of his favorite Portuguese wine, having stopped by to say "hello" to Frank before he went over to Michael's house. Andre had not shared the reason why Frank flunked out of canine police school. He did say Frank had a dark side, but she hadn't seen it.

Grace regretted the recent argument with Andre. It wouldn't do to alienate him and, somehow, an undeclared truce between them allowed them to get along enough to take care of matters. Stacking slices of a French baguette in a basket, she topped it with a plate of Gruyere cheese, olives, and hummus. Pushing the bread to one side she managed to tuck a jar of mustard into the basket. Picking up the precarious arrangement with one hand and holding a wine glass in the other, she leaned against her screen door until it opened, stepped nimbly over Frank and deftly made her way to the table without a spill. Flopping down on her chair, she put her feet up and leaned back into a canvas cushion. The big dog came up and put his furry head in her lap. Closing her eyes, she took a deep breath of night air. Did she detect scent of an early fall, she wondered. She was so tired, she felt herself drifting off.

"This is nice, but it's not going to be enough for me," she heard Andre say.

Opening one eye she squinted at him and found that, since the only light was from a lantern, she could barely make out his form in the darkness.

"Let's eat your little appetizers and walk over to the

Dolphin."

"Okay. Maybe the walk will wake me up."

"That's the spirit," Andre said. "So, what did you do about Gink?"

"I made sure she wasn't in any danger. And then I called Duane."

"Duane?"

"Sure. They're best friends. He said he'd stay the night at my dad's house. Then, in the morning, he'll take her to an outpatient alcohol program," Grace sighed. "Dad acknowledged that she had been drinking, but denied it had ever been this bad. He doesn't want to lose her, so he'll say whatever he needs to. Hopefully, she'll go willingly to the program. I'm going to stop by there every day now and check up on both of them."

After a quick clean up, they walked over to the Dolphin. The restaurant and bar had been in the center of the village for more than sixty years and was a popular hangout, as was the Tavern, for locals and folks who worked at the courthouse. It was at these neighborhood eateries that defense attorneys and prosecutors, who may have recently argued against each other in court, came to have lunch together. The probation officers tended to hang out with other probation officers and the police with other police. It was friendly, yet divided.

They sat at a table for two, Andre having steered them away from the popular bar area. She was glad he did, still upset after the attack in Hyannis Port, she didn't feel like talking with anyone. Socializing with Andre, if that's what this was, was strange enough. After checking out the familiar menu, Grace ordered rosemary chicken and a glass of sauvignon blanc, while Andre settled for fish and chips and a Cape Cod Beer.

"Tell me more about what happened in Hyannis Port."

Grace took a sip of wine. "It happened really fast. I was pushed from behind and fell. Then someone grabbed my customer's lamp and ran off with it. Unfortunately, it was dark and I couldn't see much."

"Male or female?"

"Male, I think. My dad was with me, but was asleep and

didn't see anything. Now I have to explain to Mr. Stonely that his lamp was stolen." Grace sighed. "Anything new from the official investigation?"

"The evidence from all of the crime scenes is being analyzed. We're now going on the assumption that Ben's murder and the missing Tiffany lamp are related. However, the murder scene was disturbed by a bunch of merry widows," Andre added dryly. "Crumbs were found. Oyster crackers, bread, chocolate chip cookies, cherry cough drops. Sound familiar?"

"That was all part of our picnic," Grace admitted. "The cookies were mine."

Andre smiled knowingly.

"Have any suspects been eliminated?" Grace asked, wishing to change the conversation away from her well known sweet tooth.

"There are alibis, both good and not so good, being offered up by those closest to Ben. I don't think anyone has been totally eliminated. We're trying to determine motive, which with a character like Ben, turns up a lot of potentials."

"All right, let's start with those closest to him," Grace suggested. "Although William says he doesn't want the property and inherited a large sum of cash, he seems unhappy that Imogene left Salty Cove and its contents to Ben. What's his alibi?"

"William says he was home with his wife, Morgan. Certainly not an airtight alibi, because spouses often cover up for each other. Same for Portia and Trevor. It was close to dinnertime when Ben was killed, and that's where everyone says they were. Having dinner at home."

"Speak of the devi,." Grace said, as Portia and Trevor came in the front door.

"Devils, you mean?" Andre said.

Grace had to laugh. She realized that she should be feeling uncomfortable around Andre, although she was feeling anything but. Through all of the frightful events of the past several days, Andre had been extremely vigilant, making sure Michael and Bella were safe and that she was, too. There would be time, hopefully soon, when the danger would pass, life would get back to its usual pace and she could try to figure things out. For now, she wanted to drink her wine and then maybe another and see if she could learn anything new from Andre.

"What about Ben's friend, Mason?" Grace asked. "He was threatening Ben just hours before he was shot. They were fighting over Freesia Foster."

Andre nodded. "We talked to him, at the beginning of the investigation. He said he was at a landscaping job. We checked it out with his customers, and they verified that he was on their property. But, it's not far from Salty Cove, and he could have slipped over there."

"Too bad there's not more to go on," Grace said. "He seems like such a likely candidate. What about the neighbors? Roone Seymoor showed up pretty fast when everyone was screaming, and then just as quickly, disappeared. He said he was going to tell his wife, Julia, who was making dinner. Just like everyone else was that night."

Andre's eyes were closed, as though he was shutting everything out in order to concentrate on what she was saying. Either that or he was so tired that he was falling asleep in the middle of dinner. She decided to keep on talking and see if anything she said might elicit a response.

"Roone wants to buy Salty Cove," she went on. "He thinks it's an eyesore that blocks his almost perfect view of Cape Cod Bay. He said he plans to make William an offer. Did I tell you about my suspicions of Roone and Luna Welch, another neighbor?" Andre remained silent. "Well, I think they're having an affair. I met his wife Julia. She's a friend of Audrey's. She seems like a very nice person, who's very much in love with her cheating, hunky husband."

"Hunky husband?" Andre said, opening his eyes with a snap and focusing on her with a stare that could frighten a thirsty vampire. Grace met his eyes unwaveringly.

"Ah, you were listening to me," she said. "And you'll have to agree, he is very good looking."

"Could be," Andre said with a shrug. "I hadn't thought

about it, but clearly you have."

A disturbance on the other side of the restaurant drew their attention. Portia was standing by her table, hands on her skinny hips. "You fool!" she cried. "You stupid man! What am I going to do now?"

Trevor sat with his head down, his fists clenched. He didn't respond to Portia's outburst. The normal buzz in the restaurant had come to a standstill, as everyone looked at the couple. The waitress hesitated then started towards the table, her arm out in a peace-making gesture, as if some more bread or the dessert menu might calm the situation. But, Portia lifted her glass, turned it over Trevor's head and stormed out.

"Wow," Grace said. "Every time I see those two together, they seem to be having a major disagreement. I wonder what their problem is."

"Don't know, but I think I'll have Emma talk to them again," Andre replied, signaling for the check.

"Did anyone else know you were going to go to Hyannis Port?"

"Let's see. Michael, Bella, and Duane. And my dad."

"Then someone is following you around, hoping you will lead him to the lamp."

Grace knew that what he said was true. It scared her down to her polished toenails, but she couldn't stay hidden and run a business at the same time. She had accepted an order from Tia for such a large number of painted shades that it made her nervous just thinking about it, and now she'd be checking in on her dad and Gink, too, all the time having to keep her eyes open and think about every move she made.

She and Andre walked back to Grace's house, talking about the weather, the baseball season and sailing, activities they both loved, particularly anything involving boats and swimming. When they approached Grace's house, Frank came careening around the corner, greeting them with playful leaps and a wagging tail.

"He likes it here, that's clear," Andre said. "How's it working out with Clambake?"

"Clambake has let Frank know who is top dog, in a manner of speaking," Grace replied.

"I suppose with Frank and your elusive houseguest, you'll be safe. He would have killed you by now if that was his intent," Andre observed.

"That's a comforting thought," she said.

"Seriously. You shouldn't be alone. I'd add with 'him' but I don't want to fight with you. Why won't you come over to Michaels? There's plenty of room."

Grace shook her head. "I need to be here. It's nice and quiet and there's so much work to do. I'll be safe. Don't worry. And Frank is such a sweet boy. I'll be in good company."

"That's what you think. Being sweet is one of his many disguises," Andre replied.

Grace couldn't help thinking that Frank might not be the only one around here with something to hide.

Chapter Thirty-Four

Grace ran down her stairs, her flip-flops slapping on the wooden steps. Frank raced ahead into the kitchen where Clambake, perched on a chair, was meowing his head off and demanding his breakfast be served immediately. Clambake was a very big cat and his main joy in life, non-stop petting aside, was food and plenty of it. Consequently, he was, to his obvious frustration, on a perpetual diet, that never seemed to help him lose weight, but kept him always hungry. A call to the vet might be in order soon, Grace thought. As for Frank's presence in the house, Clambake was finding a way to deal with him, mostly by staying to the high ground. As long as Frank kept away from his dish, he was okay with Frank.

After Grace fed the animals, she returned upstairs to get ready for Audrey who was picking her up so that they could go to Julia's house. Then they would all take a run around some nearby cranberry bogs. Showered and dressed, she sipped some tea while tying her running shoes, and since Frank needed to go out and get some fresh air and exercise, she picked up her binoculars and scanned the marsh. Fog was hovering, drifting and rising through the deep grasses and cattails, but blue sky was peeking through the highest clouds, promising a sunny day ahead. The osprey nest was visible above the mist, and she watched an osprey stretch its wings, to its full six-foot span, and take off, circling the marsh, dipping in and out of the morning haze.

Grace knew from her research that osprey leave Cape Cod in September and migrate southward, sometimes as far away as Brazil. The adult birds, although splitting up during their travels, usually return to their nest to fix it up with new sticks and a variety of objects they could easily find on the beach and in the marsh. Ospreys were also known to line their large nests, with oddities such as rope, bones, plastic containers and pieces of metal. Grace had read that even a Barbie Doll and a hula-hoop had been among the strange accumulations found in the tangle.

Now, as the osprey floated toward her cottage, she felt her heart quicken as the large bird, came close, circled once and soared back to the nest, where it landed and perched silently for a few minutes. Then, Grace was sure, it looked in her direction before it lifted off and headed south.

Putting her glasses away, she reached down to pet Frank, who was watching her expectantly. "We'll see her next year." Frank wagged his tail.

*****

An hour later, Audrey and Grace arrived at Julia's house, Audrey steered her Jeep into a driveway, which bordered the one that led to Salty Cove. Unlike Imogene and Ben's, it was paved and bordered by immaculate lawns and well-trimmed flowerbeds that nestled neatly in fresh wood chips. The drive ended in a wide circle, surrounded by low stonewalls. She parked under a weeping willow tree, just as a black luxury vehicle backed out of a three-car garage.

Roone Seymoor slowed his car as Grace and Audrey approached. Leaning out the window, he brushed his hair out of his eyes, smiled his perfect smile, and told them to have fun on their morning run before proceeding down the drive.

"I hope he's not going to meet Luna," Grace whispered to Audrey as Julia, dressed in black shorts, and a white T shirt, opened the door. A baseball style cap with shiny metallic sequins perched over her sleek hair, which was tied back in a ponytail.

"I just squeezed some oranges, would you like some juice before we set out?" Julia asked.

Audrey and Grace followed her down a broad, light filled hall to a spacious living room, with floor to ceiling windows and with one of the most incredible views that Grace had ever seen on Cape Cod. The house was on a hill, giving it a setting that placed it in an elevated position above the coast, from which Grace could easily see Salty Cove. Its untended scraggly roofline blocking a part of the sweeping curve of coastline, depriving the Seymoor's of a chunk of sparkling water and sandy beach.

The open floor plan of the contemporary house was impressive. Sparsely furnished, its sleek furniture was carefully positioned with a color scheme that was dominated by neutrals, primarily, gray and tan. Grace estimated the kitchen to be about the size of her barn. Striking works of art adorned the walls. Above a table that would easily seat an enormous gathering of guests hung a gorgeous crystal chandelier.

It was all a bit too perfect, Grace thought. The seemingly endless granite kitchen counters were almost bare of typical kitchen items that made a home feel lived in. It was a house that smelled of linseed oil, bleach and a stringent air freshener. No pets, no plants, and no life.

"This is incredible, "Audrey said. "I've never been in a house like this. The outside is so traditional but the inside is a total surprise."

Incredible was a good description, and she was certain that Audrey was sincere. Not wanting to reveal her own opinion, she said to Julia, "Bella told me that you have a Pairpoint Puffy. I'd love to see it."

The library was full of books so perfectly sized and arranged by color that Grace imagined they must have been bought by the yard. The Pairpoint, out of place in this sterile environment, rested on a console table in all of its bulbous glory. A riot of soft colors, like a beautiful Cape spring morning adorned a metal base.

"Nice," Audrey said.

"It's not really my taste," said Julia. "It reminds me of Easter bonnets I had to wear as a kid. But, Roone took a fancy to it. I'm sure it's a good investment."

More than good, thought Grace. Many thousands of dollars good.

"I have to agree with Roone. It's beautiful," she said, gazing longingly at the apple tree lamp, the shade painted with pink and white apple blossoms, green leaves, apples, and bumblebees.

Julia led them to some shelves of Asian pottery. "Now, this is to my taste," she explained, telling them that it was her personal collection, which she obtained after she had traveled extensively through the Far East with her first husband. "Simple and sublime."

"Why did you and your first husband travel to the East?" Audrey wanted to know.

"Robert was in the export, import business," Julia said without elaboration. "He loved traveling. He passed away very suddenly after a heart attack. After all of his travels and adventures, he died at home in his sleep.

"My husband died of a heart attack, too," Grace said, sensing a connection.

"Oh, I'm so sorry. I didn't know," Julia said. "It's so hard to lose someone you're in love with. I thank my lucky stars every day that I met Roone. He's a widow, too. His wife died suddenly while they were on a hiking trip in Nepal."

"What happened to her?" Audrey asked.

"She went off for a walk by herself, slipped and fell over the side of a cliff. It was a nightmare for Roone. Apparently there was quite an investigation into her death. He was trying to grieve, but was being questioned by the Nepalese authorities. He said he was held there for a few weeks under house arrest."

"Why?" Audrey asked. "Was he a suspect?"

"I probably shouldn't have brought this up," Julia said in a tight voice." But, yes, he was. There was a question about his whereabouts at the time she went missing. Obviously, Roone doesn't like to talk about it."

"What an awful thing to have to go through," Audrey said.

"I suppose so," Julia snapped. "I really wouldn't know, now, would I?"

Grace was startled by Julia's remark and sudden change in attitude. Audrey looked like she had been slapped. It was almost as if Audrey had made an insinuation of some kind. There was a moment of awkward silence.

Audrey cleared her throat. "We better get going. Grace and

I have to get to work. It will have to be a short run as it is."

Grace gulped the last of her orange juice and asked to use the bathroom. Julia pointed down the hall and said, "On your left."

Grace assuming she meant the first left, found herself in the master bedroom. She quickly spotted a package wrapped in Pearl's signature paper. It was the jade lamp that she had sold to Roone. About half of the paper had been ripped off, as if a child had taken a peek and decided it wasn't worth unwrapping. The card Roone had filled out was on the floor, torn in little pieces.

Why hadn't Julia opened her package? Was she that offended by the poor wrap job that Grace had managed? Although Grace barely knew the woman, she clearly had to agree with Audrey's comment that she seemed to be on edge about something.

*****

In a short while, the three women were running along the edge of a cranberry bog. Dog walkers, runners, hikers, and bird watchers regularly used the bogs, but today it was quiet. The smooth level path was easy on her feet compared with the sand and pavement that Grace usually ran on. When they came upon a small group of tourists taking pictures of the cranberry bog, Grace was reminded of the afternoon when she and Bella and the Merry Widows had driven to Salty Cove for a walk and a sunset picnic, oblivious of what dreadful sights awaited them.

The temperature was inching up and by the time they finished and were back at Julia's they were all panting. Julia ran inside and brought a bottle of chilled mineral water for each of them. When a man riding a mower, came into view, she said. "I've brought one for Mason too. He must be broiling."

Grace thought back to the day of the osprey rescue and her encounter with Mason and Roone and remembered her surprise at the peculiar sight of the sophisticated antique collector and the rough man with the unsavory background. Why, she had wondered then, with all the landscaping professionals around, would anyone hire him?

Julia must have intuited what she was thinking because she said she and Roone had met Mason through Imogene and Ben. They did have professional landscapers, of course, but for smaller jobs they often called on Mason, assuming he could use the money. Furthermore, he had grown up in the neighborhood, so everyone knew him.

What everyone in the neighborhood most likely also knew was that Mason, like Ben, had been in and out of jail for a myriad of offenses.

"How long has he been working for you?" Audrey asked.

"A few weeks. Roone thought it would be good to help him out. Mason has been so upset by Ben's murder," she paused and took a sip of water. "I sometimes think that it could have been me who discovered Ben's body. I often brought cookies or brownies to Ben and Imogene."

Grace had a hard time imaging Julia carrying goodies to the neighbors. Somehow, it rang false to her, although she didn't know why. Perhaps she was being cranky because Audrey and Julia had left her far behind during their run. She'd have to work hard to keep up with these two.

"I'm glad I wasn't home when you and those older ladies discovered the body," Julia continued. "Roone told me it was an awful scene."

Grace thought she picked up a slight accusatory tone in Julia's voice. 'You and *those* ladies.' Was there something in her tone that suggested that Grace or the Merry Widows were somehow responsible for Ben's death? But that was absurd. Julia seemed to be irritable and paranoid, too. Clearly Bens' death had affected so many of them. This neighborhood, where he grew up, would be particularly susceptible to fear and suspicions.

"Mason didn't come to the service at the funeral home," Grace mused, remembering that Mason had dropped Freesia off. It occurred to her that Mason might have had time to break into Salty Cove, since that had happened during the wake. Maybe Mason was looking for a Tiffany lamp, instead of paying his respects to his best friend.

"I assume it was too much for him to handle," Julia said.

"When Robert died I was a basket case. I could barely attend his service."

Grace nodded in sympathy. This time, she had to admit she knew exactly what Julia was talking about.

*****

After Audrey dropped her off at home, Grace saw dishes piled in the sink, and knew that Felix had returned while she was out. She certainly didn't miss him, but he was becoming more like a ghost than the all-pervading houseguest he had been at the beginning of his stay. Ever since he had found her rummaging in his room, he had been keeping a very low profile.

When Grace opened her top desk drawer and saw that her usually tidy assortment of pens and papers was now a disorganized mess, it took her less than a moment to settle on Felix as the most likely person to have poked around there, looking for who knows what. Why, she wondered had she ever agreed to let him stay at her house? Andre was right; she didn't know anything about him, other than the fact that he was a friend of Guy Sutter. Perhaps she had better call Guy, who would be at work now, and see if she could find out more about Felix.

"Felix was a fraternity brother of mine," Guy said, after a brief exchange of pleasantries. "Is there a problem?"

Grace filled Guy in on her houseguest's activities. And how, what she had thought was a tedious houseguest, had become someone far more than annoying. She didn't like the idea of him messing around in her personal space.

"I'm sorry, Grace," Guy said. "I never imagined that he would be such a pain in the neck. I always considered him a bit strange, but harmless. Did I mention that he's an accountant?"

"No," Grace said. "He's been vague about what he does for a living, but I have to say, I'm surprised."

"Felix likes people to think he's a journalist. Sorry about that. I'll be more careful next time."

"There won't be a next time, Guy," Grace said. Of that, she was certain.

Chapter Thirty-Five

Grace loaded up her car with lamps, boxes, ribbons, and shades that she had removed from her home work area and drove the four minute drive from her cottage on Freezer Road to Pearl's, where the 'OPEN' sign was hanging prominently on the front door.

As she went down the hallway, she peered into the chandelier room, and seeing Michael on his ladder, maneuvering a long handled duster among the crystals, she groaned. "Duane could have done that, you know."

"I know," Michael told her, but I was watching re-runs of Downton Abbey last night, and I saw the scene in the beginning with the feather duster cleaning the chandelier, and I was inspired."

Grace sighed and silently reminded herself not to get involved in fruitless discussions about ladders. "I stopped and picked up some bagels and cream cheese for when we get hungry later," she told him as Bella popped up from behind her counter, looking fresher than she had in days.

"What do you mean later?" she demanded, "I could go for some bagels now."

"Me, too," Michael said, leaning his ladder against the wall.

"Isn't this lovely?" Bella said, cleaning a large clear glass bottle. The customer wants me to make a lamp out of it. She plans to fill it with pebbles and stones, porcelain mushrooms and tiny woodland creatures."

"That is a beautiful bottle," Grace agreed. "I think a simple white shade with some delicate leaf paintings around the edge would be perfect."

"Speaking of woodlands and leaves and such, right after my bagel break, I'm going to plant some flowers in the front window boxes," Michael said. "Those dead ones have got to go. Nothing gets done around here unless I do it myself."

As Michael traipsed to the back porch to get plants, watering can, and a trowel, Grace marveled at how things were coming together at Pearl's. Bella was repairing lamps, Michael tidying up and taking charge of everyone, and now, Duane was coming in the door, wearing a tie-dyed t-shirt, carrying a bag from Dunkin Donuts. Sitting down at her pine table, paints and brushes ready at her fingertips, she decided that after they had their coffee and snacks, she'd tell them about the order she had agreed to for the Falmouth inn. She'd thought about it last night and was feeling more confident. She had some ideas about how they could get it done.

It was almost like old times.

*****

Customers streamed into the shop throughout the afternoon, including Clay who stopped by to see if they were serving refreshments to celebrate the re-opening. Roaming from room to room, he opened drawers, peered into cabinets and generally stuck his nose in places it had no business being. Grace caught up with him, his tall frame bent over as he was surveying the contents of the refrigerator.

"You're not likely to find any shades in there, Clay," Grace greeted him. "And there won't be any goodies until we have an official re-opening party in a couple of weeks."

Clay closed the door. "No harm in checking," he muttered, in his nasally voice. "If I do say so, Pearl's looks charming. Not the same atmosphere, of course, but very nice."

Grace assumed that that was the best compliment she would get from Clay, who was as stingy with his praise as he was with his wallet.

"I need your assistance," he told her. "I've got a new client. She just came back from a safari and is very excited about animal prints. I've proposed a jungle savanna theme for her sunroom. A nice shade for her brass lamp would be a good place to start. What have you got in the way of jungle fabric?"

When Grace pulled out three fabrics that she thought would work, he said, "These are just what I'm looking for. I'll bring her in next week and I'll let her pick out something. Oh my! Do I see something special over there?" In a matter of seconds he was standing in front of a lamp with a reverse painted shade. "Is that an African theme I see?"

"Yes, but not safari exactly," Grace said. "Egyptian. See the camels?"

"I do. I doubt my client will know the difference," he told her. It's so gorgeous, and the salmon, blue, and tan colors are perfect. I'll convince her to love it."

"I almost forgot to mention it, but a woman named Tia Jones called," Michael interrupted them. "She was quite brusque and wanted to know how things were coming with her special order. When I told her she must be mistaken because no one had mentioned any such order to me, she became rather angry and said you should call her immediately. She hung up on me, without even a goodbye."

Grace cringed. It was the type of cringe in which her stomach churned and tossed unpleasantly. As if reading her mind, Clay asked about Tia's order. "How are we coming with that?" he asked.

"Fine." It was a stretch of the truth, but after all, no use telling Clay that she hadn't started on it yet. In fact, when she came to think about it, there was no use telling Clay anything at all.

*****

Grace sat down in Bella's workspace. In just a day or so, Bella had managed to re-create the disorder that once prevailed upstairs. Although Bella declared that she was completely organized, disarray and minor chaos ruled her day. Grace worried about her tripping over drills and cords, but as part of her new non-controlling strategy, she'd given up trying to tell Bella what to do, knowing that she wouldn't listen anyway.

"Grace, I almost forgot to mention that we are invited to Portia and Trevor's house for some drinks and a family meeting," Bella said.

"We?"

"Well, me, but I could use a ride. I'm pretty sure they will be talking about Salty Cove. It will probably be very helpful for our investigation. By the way, where are we with that?"

"Nothing yet, I'm afraid," Grace said, figuring that was the best way to keep Bella from asking questions, besides being the truth. No one seemed to know anything, despite the fact that Andre and other officers were working long hours. "Do you think we should go through your house together, just to make sure we haven't overlooked anything?' Grace asked.

Bella gave her a sideways glance, and then returned to her glass lamp. "Hmm, I suppose we should," she said. "We'll talk about that later. In any case, you can pick me up and drive me to Portia's right after work, if you don't mind."

It appeared to Grace that her accompanying Bella to Portia and Trevor's house was a done deal. Maybe it wouldn't be as dreadful as she imagined.

"It's so wonderful to be back at work," Bella continued. "And our Michael, bless his heart. The commotion of the move made him nervous. It upset his neat and tidy world," she chuckled. "I wouldn't admit it to him, of course, but, all in all, bunking with him has been a pleasurable experience. But, I'm ready to go home now."

"What does André think?"

"He thinks I should stay right where I am, with Michael. I haven't decided yet, but I told him I wouldn't be alone. "

"You won't?" Grace asked, curious as to whom Bella could possibly be referring. Perhaps Portia and William had arranged for someone to stay with her.

"Owen, Ben's son, is staying at my house," Bella told her. "Oh dear, did I forget to mention that to you?"

Grace was so flabbergasted she could barely choke out her question. "Owen is staying at your house? No, you didn't mention that."

Grace had to wonder what else Bella might have forgotten to tell her. It seemed that Bella was full of surprises these last few days.

Chapter Thirty-Six

Grace parked a few steps from the grand entrance to Portia and Trevor's lovely, yet rather ostentatious south side home.

"Nice," Grace said.

"Portia has done well for herself, marrying Trevor," Bella agreed. "He's been able to provide for her in style."

Grace filled Bella in on the argument at the Dolphin between Portia and Trevor. "Portia seems to have the upper hand when it comes to him. What do you think?"

"Trevor is more reserved than Portia. I do believe he tries hard to keep her happy."

"Maybe that's not possible."

Bella nodded in agreement and stopped to adjust a large red earring. More dressed up then Grace had ever seen her, she wore a red checkered shirt and denim skirt, with white sandals.

"I'm not sure why I was invited to this family meeting," she said. "But I do have a lot to tell them about the provenance of the Tiffany lamp. But, let's see what they're up to first."

Pausing on the neat gravel walk to admire the extensive gardens and lawn, Grace reached down to cup a brilliant late blooming rose in her hand and take a breath of sweetness.

"Watch out! There's a snake!" Bella exclaimed, pointing to a nearby rock.

Grace pulled her hand quickly away from the flower. "Oh, look. It's a harmless baby northern black racer. That's one thing I don't miss from living in California. Rattlesnakes lurking in the hills."

"There could be rattlers here for cocktails," Bella let out a hearty laugh. "And now," she said briskly, "Let's see what the Walwyn family has summoned us here for on this lovely day."

*****

They were soon seated in the living room furnished as if a set designer had just plumped the final pillow and left the stage. The ornamental design of the slipcovers that had been repeated in the drapery, complimented the tables topped with Limoges figurines and a cozy gathering of Herenden rabbits.

To her surprise, Trevor handed Grace a glass of wine as soon as she was seated on the plushy loveseat, while Morgan and William, who had preceded them, were sitting quietly side by side on a matching sofa. When they were all settled with their drinks, Trevor, who apparently had been drinking before his guests arrived, clumsily got to his feet raised his glass and declared, "Here's to the Walwyn family. A family of scoundrels, secrets, intrigue, and scandal."

He took a big swig of his wine. Grace, shocked, but not knowing what she should do, took a healthy sip of her chardonnay. She wondered if this was the way things usually went at these family get-togethers.

"Trevor, sit down and be quiet," Portia said. She gazed around at all of them and smiled. "Let's try another toast, shall we? Here's to husbands with their own secrets, intrigues, and scandals!"

Grace peered over the rim of her glass and saw shock and distress on the faces of William and Morgan. As for Bella, her expression registered alarm.

Once again, Trevor lifted his glass and opened his mouth, but Bella waved her arm and got slowly to her feet, before any sound emerged. After a brief hesitation, and appearing to be calm and composed, she offered a toast of her own. "Here's to the Walwyn family. A family I've known for many years and love very much."

Grace clicked her glass with Bella as a sign of what she hoped would signal her support. She took another sip of wine and saw Bella do the same. At this rate, she'd be tipsy before she knew it. Better have a few of the crackers that were on the far side of the coffee table, but they were out of her reach, and no one was eating them, much less passing them around.

William laughed nervously and without getting up, raised his glass. "Don't all families have their little secrets?" he said. "I'll second Bella's toast. Here's to the Walwyn family that I'm fond of."

Uh, oh, thought Grace. The conversation was entering pretty nasty territory. What had brought on these sarcastic toasts? Had Trevor discovered Imogene's habit of stealing expensive items? Or was he referring to Owens's unexpected existence? And to what was Portia alluding? What secrets did Trevor have that would be serious enough to include intrigue and scandal? It was likely no one had missed William's editing of Bella's toast. Fond was a long way from love.

She tried to signal Bella, who was nearest to the cheese, to pass it to her. But it was obvious to her, by the rise in color on Bella's cheeks that she was fuming and unlikely to pass crackers or anything else, at the moment.

When the room fell into an uneasy silence, Grace drank again, nearly emptying her glass. Trevor swooped in and topped it off.

"All right, we've all had our moment," Portia said. "Now let's get on with it, shall we? It appears that our new nephew, Owen, has proven his identity to the powers that be."

"That's what I have been informed," William replied.

"And now, are we to be cast aside by this stranger, Ben's secret son?"

"I had a thought just now," Morgan piped up, pausing to take a sip. Grace anticipating another toast managed to slide her glass closer, without spilling a drop. "Maybe there are others? I mean, Ben was in his forties. It's certainly a possibility."

Portia let out a choking sound. The rest of the family gasped. Then, angry voices took over, competing to be heard. Trevor roved around filling glasses, and Grace sensing an opportunity got up, circled the table, seized the appetizers, and returned with them to her seat.

"Grace, dear, all you had to do was ask," Portia said. Now everyone was quiet again, watching Grace, who normally, would have been horrified to be called out by her hostess. But her need for food displaced any humiliation she might have felt. She took a second helping and passed the basket to Morgan, who passed it on to William.

"Look, it doesn't change anything," William said, cupping a handful of crackers in his hand. "However many children Ben may have had, it won't change a thing for any of us." And then, as though speaking to himself, "He must have told someone. I'll bet Mom knew."

"Well, isn't that nice if she did," Portia said, her voice thick with irony. "It would have been good of her to let us know. We're the ones who have been taking care of Ben, one scrape after another, for what seems like eons. And now Owen will get Salty Cove, which is worth a pretty penny." She held out her glass for Trevor to refill. "William, what can we do? You're a lawyer."

"I'm a criminal lawyer," William cleared his throat, "but, remember, Mom left us quite a bit of money. The house was to go to Ben. It was only after he died, that we would have inherited the estate. We will surely be made to look greedy in court, out to keep a young man from his inheritance."

Portia exploded. "Greedy? Us? We have bills to pay too! Why should a complete stranger get anything?" She placed her napkin on the table. "We need to get the property and sell the damn place!"

"As long as Owen is alive, our chances are slim to none," William said, flushing. "Sorry, poor choice of words, after what happened to our poor Ben. I misspoke. Forgive me."

"It's all right, William," said Bella, who had been strangely silent following her toast, She hadn't mentioned that she and Imogene both knew about Owen, not to mention the problems with the provenance of the Tiffany. In turn, no one had mentioned the troubles at Pearl's, or asked her how she was faring after her terrible experience in her house. "I do have something I'd like to share with you all," she said at last.

"Portia, I thought you didn't want to sell Salty Cove?" William said, ignoring Bella. "A few days ago, you said you wanted to keep it and upgrade it. Keep it in the family for sentimental reasons."

"I've changed my mind," she said sharply.

"Trevor, who had been downing glass after glass of wine, and had, at some point, switched to bourbon and water, suddenly pounded his fist on the table next to where he sat, causing the glass top to tremble, as though it had been the victim of a small earthquake. The Limoges figures rattled precariously. "Look, we want Salty Cove, and we want to sell! Like you said, the neighbor, Roone, is ready to make an offer."

William held up a hand. "We may get nothing, so you better be prepared. It's not like you two need the money."

Portia suddenly burst into tears, pressing her face into her calico napkin. "We're broke!"

William looked at his sister as if she had lost her mind. "Come on Portia. By most anyone's standards you're filthy rich and recently inherited a tidy sum. Trevor, can't you talk to her?" he added irritably.

"Things aren't always as they seem," Trevor replied cryptically, running a hand through his white hair.

Portia leaped out of her chair. "Tell them what you did!"

Trevor sidled over to the fireplace and rested an arm on the mantle. "I borrowed money from the bank, and made some unfortunate investments."

"You embezzled money from your clients!" Portia shouted. "And now we're broke, and you are going to jail."

"My lawyer tells me that if I can offer to pay restitution, I might get probation instead of jail. After all, I didn't hurt anyone."

"What about us?" Portia demanded.

"Us? I did it all for you, love." Trevor said, and then excused himself as chimes announced the arrival of someone at the front door.

"I invited the Seymoor's to stop by," Portia explained, swiftly regaining her composure. "William, I know you don't approve, but I thought it might be best if we all talked about the possibilities of selling the property to them."

"You shouldn't have invited him here!" William exploded. Portia gave her brother a 'get a hold of yourself' look, as the new guests entered the room and greetings were exchanged. Roone threaded his way through the group, politely shaking everyone's hand, a pleasant smile on his face, while Julia hung back and barely nodded to the group.

Bella asked for some coffee for herself and Grace. Roone accepted a glass of wine. Julia asked for ice water.

"I would like to say again, how very sorry we are for the losses you have been through," Roone said softly. "It was sad when Imogene passed away, but what happened to Ben is beyond words." He looked directly at William. "We heard he was getting his life together and was going to get married. Such a tragedy."

"You want to talk about tragedy?" Portia said. "He was going to marry that woman, Freesia Foster. We've known her for years. I doubt she'd have been a positive influence."

Julia accepted her glass of water. "Are you talking about that appallingly repulsive woman that was so disruptive at the funeral home? No, she would have been a disaster for Ben."

Grace was surprised at the degree of anger directed toward Freesia. And why would Julia care? Did she even know Freesia?

There followed a discussion that involved various scenarios that might happen regarding the future ownership of Salty Cove. Portia added, "One more problem Ben left for us to tidy up."

Grace saw Julia nod her head. So that was it. Julia was doing her best to agree with everything Portia said. What better way to make certain that Portia would view her favorably if, by some stroke of fortune, Portia and William would end up with Salty Cove?

Bella tried unsuccessfully to tell the family about the provenance of the missing Tiffany lamp, but she was ignored. The evening's focus seemed to be on the Walwyn family's legal matters. Grace began to feel sleepy and fed up with the conversation, which drifted into areas that had little to do with her. She stared at the herd of porcelain bunnies and tried to figure a way to get away from this insufferable group. She peered over at Bella who was finishing up her coffee.

As if reading Grace's mind, Bella said, "This has been a lovely evening, as always, Portia, but we must go. Ready, Grace?"

'We're leaving, too," Roone said. "You all should know that I have to have that property. Hopefully, we can work something out soon, but if we can't, I'll be negotiating with Owen."

On the way back to the village Bella said, "I wanted to tell them all about the Tiffany lamp, but they never gave me a chance."

""It was hard to get in a word with all of the toasts, insults, and threats," Grace replied. "I feel lucky we got out of there in one piece. Family gatherings can be so much fun."

"Indeed, they can be," Bella chuckled.

"Bella, do you think Portia or Trevor would be capable of murder?"

"Nothing would surprise me now," Bella told her, and Grace made a mental note to find out more about Trevor's finances. If he was facing jail, and the loss of huge sums of money, it could be a motive for murder.

Chapter Thirty-Seven

Grace drove to Hyannis early the next morning, after having woken during the night, tossing and turning, stressed out by Tia's order for the custom shades. When would she possibly find the time to get started, let alone finish the job? She had to get organized, and figure out her priorities, or her reputation and that of the shop would be ruined. Despite her stress she had realized, in the wee hours of the night, that before anything else, there was one person she needed to talk to. One person who knew Ben Walwyn very well, and might know something about a valuable Tiffany lamp.

Although it was early, the road was thick with tourists on their way to claim a parking spot at the beach. Tired of the busy roads, Grace ducked down a side street lined with houses of various vintages, some with newly mowed lawns, a few with dry, scrubby grass, and many littered with brightly colored children's toys. A commotion, from the direction of a condominium complex, drew her attention. She noticed a group of preteen boys speeding around the entrance on skateboards, as a battered, dirty, gray car attempted to maneuver into the driveway around them.

"Get out of my way!" a small woman with hair like a birds nest cried, leaning on her horn. "Can't you clowns see that you're blocking the driveway? You kids think you own the road? I've got a load of groceries here."

Grace recognized the sharp voice of Freesia Foster, Ben's ex-girlfriend, who was still leaning on her horn as she careened into the complex. Grace turned in behind the vehicle, and slipped between the boys, their boards, and a couple of tween girls deep in conversation. She followed the car until Freesia, roughly scraping the side of a concrete wall, brought her sagging vehicle to a grinding stop. As Grace pulled in behind her, a Red Socks bumper sticker caught her attention.

Freesia fumbled in her backseat. Then, carrying a plastic grocery bag, she sauntered toward a two story building, sorting through a set of jangling keys and muttering to herself. Her hair, now a canary yellow, and listing in four unexpected directions, flew upwards as she abruptly stopped, turned around and stared in Grace's direction. She hesitated for a split second, and then, shuffled over to Grace's car.

"I'm not on probation anymore, Ms. Tolliver," she said. "You live around here, or are you just following me?"

Grace, startled by the woman's frank assessment and trying fervently to come up with something plausible to say, finally stammered, "Hey, Freesia. I want to talk to you. It has nothing to do with probation. I saw that you were pretty upset at Ben Walwyn's wake."

Freesia cocked her head to the side. "Yeah? Could be. What were you doing there? Why are you asking me about Ben?"

"Well...we met shortly before he died. I'm not a P.O. anymore. I own a lamp shop now. Ben came by the shop the day he ..."

"Lamp shop? What would Ben be doing in a lamp shop?"

"He came to see an old friend," Grace said, beginning to wish that she hadn't decided, in the middle of last night, to come and see Freesia. What had she been thinking? Now, she was on the defensive answering an angry woman's questions.

Freesia swayed as a bottle fell out of her bag and crashed heavily to the ground. "Oh, no! My gin!" she cried as the clear liquid trickled toward a grimy metal grate, spewing the scent of alcohol into the air. "Look what you've done! Now what am I supposed to do?"

"Here, I'll help you," Grace said, feeling she had to, now that she had come this far, but certainly not appreciating being blamed for something she had no part in. Besides, it was clear to her now, that Freesia was intoxicated. Still swaying, Freesia reached down and tried to pick up her grocery bag, dropping her keys into the puddle of gin and broken glass. A moment later, holding up a finger that was sliced and bleeding, she let out a wail that could be heard in South Boston.

"We'd better take a look at your finger," Grace said, picking up the rest of the contents of the bag; an apple, a bag of chips, and a can of soda and handing them to Freesia before gingerly picking up the larger shards of glass and wrapping them in the damp grocery bag. "Where's your house?"

When Freesia pointed a bloody finger at a first floor end unit, Grace stooped and picked up a set of keys secured together by a ring that was embossed with the initials BW, and had the dual function of being a handy bottle opener. She passed the clanging keys to Freesia, who opened the door, as an orange cat made a bid for freedom. Running to her kitchen sink, where after a few minutes of rinsing and more than a few moans and groans, she held her finger out to Grace, who was depositing the paper bag with the broken bottle in the trash.

"Is it bad? Do I need stitches?" Freesia asked, absent-mindedly patting the head of a black kitten that had jumped on the counter.

"It doesn't look too serious. Do you have any bandages?" Grace asked her.

"In the medicine cabinet in the bathroom," Freesia said, pointing to a door that was steps from the kitchen. Grace opened a medicine cabinet, chock full of over- the- counter meds and poked around until she found some bandages and a tube of antibiotic cream. There was a multi-leveled shelf next to the sink, crowded with a variety of shampoos and conditioners, a large basket that contained an assortment of cosmetics and jewelry, including the sparkling bracelet that Bella had observed at Ben's service. She briefly considered browsing further in the basket, but snooping in Freesia's bathroom was not something she was willing to do.

When she returned to the living room, Freesia was lying on a tattered suede couch, an arm resting on her forehead, a white cat resting on her lap. Holding out her hand for Grace to bandage the cut, which did not seem to be more than a superficial wound. Grace obliged, by applying a dollop of antibiotic cream and wrapping the bandage snugly around Freesias finger.

Once finished, Grace surveyed the room. The couch, draped with Freesia's prone form, took up most of one wall, a dreadful shade of turquoise, paired with a bright red baseboard. A chair that matched the sofa, a television the size of a bed sheet, and assorted tables stuffed the remainder of the small apartment. And there were cats everywhere. Grace had never been in a room with so many cats since she volunteered at the Brewster animal shelter. The blinds were drawn and a distinct odor of multiple cat boxes permeated the closed space. In the gloomy, cave like space, Grace couldn't help but think she might have wandered into a lion's den.

"I think I should lie down for a while," Freesia said. "I feel dizzy from the loss of blood. My boyfriend will be here soon, so, you should probably go."

"Did you say your boyfriend?" Grace asked. "I thought you were engaged to Ben."

Freesia closed her eyes and rubbed her forehead. "Of course I was engaged to Ben, but he died, and I don't like to be alone. So, now I'm back with Mason."

"Back with Mason? You mean Ben's friend?" Grace said, feigning ignorance.

"That's what I said."

"Did they still hang out together?"

"Oh sure, but they didn't always get along."

"Why was that? Was it because of you?"

Freesia rolled over onto to her side so that she faced Grace. Her expression was dark and defiant. "What's with all of the questions?" she demanded in a harsh voice. "Didn't I tell you to go?"

Before Grace could come up with an answer, Freesia threw the cat off her lap and rising, started for her, her fists clenched.

Grace, momentarily stung by Freesia's sudden turn from placid couch potato to madwoman, jumped from her chair, her heart pounding, as Freesia confronted her. She was well aware of Freesia and her criminal record, but she had never encountered her when she was drinking. Freesia had a history of fights in bars, restaurants, and even when housed in the Barnstable Correctional Facility. Hadn't she assaulted another inmate without provocation? And now, she stood in front of Grace, her hair, having come loose, tumbling about her head like a hurricane.

Grace realized that she let her guard down. She was well aware how unpredictable someone under the influence could be. Freesia could clearly change her mood in a second. So, she said the first thing that came to her mind.

"I was just trying to make conversation, while I made sure that you were okay. I didn't want to leave you alone while you were feeling dizzy."

Freesia stopped in her tracks, blinked, and stumbled back to the couch. "You're right. I shouldn't be alone," she muttered. "Maybe you should stay until Mason comes home." She looked at her tiny bandage and having apparently accepted Grace's flimsy explanation, continued the conversation as if she hadn't just about scared the living daylights out of Grace. "Now, what was I saying? Oh yes, Ben and Mason were like brothers. They drank hard, and fought hard. Sometimes, I was with Ben and sometimes I was with Mason. When I had a fight with Ben, I would be with Mason. And vicey- versa." Freesia glared at Grace. "It's not as if Ben didn't have plenty of other girlfriends. Mason, too. But, I was special to both of them."

"When did you and Ben get together?" Grace, still standing, her heartbeat slowing, asked, hoping that Freesia would tell her more. But, to be on the safe side, given Freesia's rapid change of moods, she noted the proximity of a very large vase. Just in case.

"You mean this last time?"

"Yes."

"Let's see. I guess it was a few months ago." Freesia peered over her arm at Grace. "If you're going to sit there asking me a bunch of questions, I think I'm gonna need a drink. You want one?"

"Sure, got any ice tea?"

"What?"

"Never mind, water will be fine."

Freesia sauntered over to the kitchen, bent down and pulled a bottle of gin from a lower cabinet and two large glasses out of the sink, rinsed them, and poured about a cupful of gin in each one. Then she retrieved a bottle of tonic from the fridge and poured about a teaspoonful into each glass. Not bothering to add ice, she took a healthy sip out of one, and handed the other to Grace, her pinky finger outstretched as if they were at a tea party. What the hell, Grace thought. If it puts Freesia at ease, I'll play along. And the truth was, after Freesia's display of aggression, maybe a sip or two of gin wasn't such a bad idea, even if it was only nine o'clock in the morning. She took a sip of the concoction and choked.

"So, what were you asking me about Ben?" Freesia asked.

After another moment or two of coughing and choking, Grace stammered. "Did you get back together with him around the time his mother, Imogene, died?"

Freesia took another drink of gin and sauntered back to the couch. "It was after Imogene died. I felt sorry for him, losing his mother and all. I wanted to help him through his difficult time."

Grace wasn't buying Freesia's self-described selflessness. What did she hope to gain? Grace watched as Freesia slipped back to her horizontal position on the couch, her head resting on one armrest, her tiny feet, clad in silver tennis shoes, on another. She took big gulps of gin, and was already nearing the bottom of the glass.

As a probation officer, Grace had conducted hundreds, if not thousands of interviews, but this one was far from the norm. She took another sip of gin, hoping to get into the proper spirit. Several questions were blazing through her mind. One thing was certain, she needed to find out as much as she could, especially since Freesia seemed to have settled down and was not objecting to their chat.

"Salty Cove is such a lovely old place," she said. "Were you looking forward to living there after you and Ben were married?"

"Yeah. I'm quite artistic and I was looking forward to doing some decorating. Fixing up the place. Kinda like I've done here. You know?"

Grace looked around the room, in which she could see no sign of anything remotely artistic or decorative, but said, "Yes. You've done a beautiful thing with this place."

"I'm very talented," Freesia agreed, polishing off her drink.

"I like decorating, too," Grace told her. "My shop is in Barnstable Village. "Weren't you there two nights ago?"

Freesia shot up straight. "What are you saying? I don't go to Barnstable Village unless I have to go to court." She stared at the floor, busily twirling a lock of hair. "Or something," she added.

"Yes, of course," Grace said. It was unlikely that Freesia would admit trying to break into Pearl's, but she decided to ask anyway. The Red Sox sticker and the make of the car were similar to what she and Felix had recalled seeing, but Freesia's answer hadn't helped at all. Still, there were a couple of things she would take a close look at on her way out. Was Freesia's windshield wiper missing?

I've been to Salty Cove," Grace said. "The furnishings are really nice. Do you remember any antique lamps, by chance?"

"Ben showed me a lot of stuff in that place," Freesia said, lounging back against the couch and burping loudly. "He said some of it was very valuable and that we might sell some of it to finance our B&B. There was one lamp he said would make us rich if we sold it. Are you sure my finger is gonna be all right? Maybe we should call 911?"

"No, I think you'll be fine," Grace assured her, her heart starting to race again. "What kind of lamp was it?"

"A very pretty one. He said someone famous made it. Can you imagine?" Freesia muttered. "That reminds me, I need to get a lawyer. That lamp should be mine, along with everything else in that old house. After all, we were engaged. Ben's brother William usually helps me with my legal matters, but I don't think he'll be interested in helping me now, do you?"

"No, I suppose not," Grace said, knowing that would be a most unlikely scenario. "It would be a conflict of interest."

Changing moods and subject again, Freesia looked slyly at Grace. "Since it was your fault I dropped my bottle," she said, "Do you think you could get me some more gin before Mason returns? I'd go to the store, but I probably shouldn't because of my finger."

"Sure, whatever," Grace said, not meaning it, but aware that Freesia would most likely forget their entire conversation, in a minute or two. "Before I go to the store, can you tell me anything about the valuable lamp that Ben mentioned? What it looked like?"

"It had...some kind of insect, I think," Freesia broke off and closed her eyes, toppling over like a rag doll.

"Rats!" Grace said. "Freesia! Did you have a fight with Ben? Did you kill him?" Grace asked, moving swiftly to the couch, knowing she had little time before Freesia was dead to the world.

"No, I...." Freesia responded.

"What did Ben do with the dragonfly lamp?" Grace demanded, losing patience.

"He gave it to someone to keep."

"Freesia! Who killed Ben?"

"I guess someone... who was... mad at him," Freesia sputtered, tucked her hands under her chin and closed her eyes.

Grace had hoped for more, but she knew that Freesia had most likely spoken the simple truth.

*****

Placing a pillow under Freesia's head, Grace watched as she settled into a healthy snore. Still, she decided to stay with her awhile and make sure she was all right.

Grace felt she had been close to discovering information that might be helpful in finding out about Ben's killer and the valuable Tiffany lamp. Freesia knew both Ben and Mason very well. The three of them had grown up together, and their lives were romantically interwoven. Surely, there were rivalries and jealousies that still existed. It was clear now that Freesia knew about the lamp, and that it was very valuable. There was no doubt in her mind that if Freesia knew, Mason would, too.

Freesia's key chain was inscribed with Ben's initials. Did any of the many keys on the ring open doors to Salty Cove? If so, had she been in the house, and removed the Tiffany? Or, had she given the keys to Mason to do the deed? Freesia was a person of extreme mood changes, an alcohol problem, and a criminal record. It wouldn't do to underestimate her.

Grace was deciding what to do next, when there was a loud knock on the door. Her heart thumped. Mason? She didn't think he'd be happy finding Freesia passed out and a former probation officer on the premises.

Another knock. Grace hesitated, and then, bracing herself, opened the door to find Andre standing there with officer Gelb right behind him.

"Oh, hi," she said, trying hard not to show her surprise. "What are you doing here?"

"I saw your car outside." He looked over her shoulder at Freesia sprawled on the couch. "I hope there aren't any dead bodies in here."

"Very funny," Grace answered.

"We're here to interview Freesia Foster about Ben Walwyn." Gelb interjected. "I guess that's her over there?"

"That's her. She's had a bit too much to drink," Grace said. "She'll come around shortly. I have to be going."

"She's not the only one who's been drinking. Is that alcohol on your breath?" Andre asked, leaning close enough that she could feel his breath on her cheek.

"Um,...I'll tell you about it some other time. I've got to get to Pearl's."

As she left, Grace heard Gelb, trying to wake Freesia up, an attempt which apparently succeeded because she shrieked. She almost felt sorry for the officers. Interviewing Freesia was not going to be easy.

"I'll call you later," Andre said, as Grace picked up her purse. "Then maybe you can tell me why you're here with my interview subject passed out on her couch."

"Sure, absolutely," Grace said, closing the door behind her. But the truth was, when it came down to it, there was nothing sure or absolute about the events of the past week.

Chapter Thirty-Eight

Her head spinning from the after effects of her morning spent with Freesia, not to mention the gin cocktail she'd drank, Grace entered Pearl's through the back door. On her way out of the apartment complex, she looked at Freesia's car and saw that the left windshield wiper was broken. So, it had to have been Freesia who tried to break into Pearl's. Or maybe, it occurred to Grace, it was Mason who had been driving her car.

Bella was talking to someone in the main part of the shop. Grace did not get a happy feeling when she recognized the now all too familiar voice of her houseguest.

"I'm going to the outer Cape to do some research for an article I'm writing for my class," she heard him say.

"Wellfleet is lovely," Bella replied. "I'm sure you'll enjoy yourself."

"Good morning, Bella,... and Felix," she interrupted them, determined to take this opportunity to confront him about snooping in her desk.

"Hey Grace," Felix said, removing a notebook from the pocket of his jeans. "I was in the area again and wanted to come by and take another look at your shop. I think my story about it is coming along pretty well. My instructor says I need more details. Can I look around?"

She wanted to say 'no' but couldn't think of a good reason to bar Felix from walking around Pearl's.

"Did you talk to Guy recently?" she asked him.

"Yeah," he said, adjusting the brim of his baseball cap. "He called me about half an hour ago and said you were pissed at me and that I better come see you. I didn't mess with any of your stuff. I needed a pen is all." He hesitated. "Just so you know, I didn't mention to Guy about you snooping in my things."

Grace was relieved that this would hopefully be the last conversation with her houseguest. She was no longer certain if he was clueless, lazy, or simply the houseguest from hell, but in any case, she would be happy to see him go. Besides, she didn't keep anything valuable in her desk. She was partly responsible, because she said he could stay with her, and he had caught her sneaking around in his closet, even though, it was, after all, *her* closet and she couldn't be too careful these days. She took in his scruffy blue jeans; his rumpled tee shirt, and his tanned feet protruding from thick sandals and reminded herself that today, Felix would be busy up in Wellfleet, which meant that he would not be hanging around her cottage. Soon he would be out of her life forever.

Michael hovered over her watching as she mixed her watercolors, keeping an eagle eye on Felix as he wandered around the shop. A few minutes passed, and Felix, having apparently satisfied his curiosity, waved to them, and left the store.

"He is a strange sort of fellow. But, I think pretty harmless. Don't you Grace?"

"Harmless? I wouldn't go that far," she said dryly. "My house is beginning to resemble an osprey nest, one big mess, thanks to Felix."

"Speaking of birds," Bella interrupted, "Are you still a volunteer osprey observer, Grace?"

"I am, but I think they're gone for the season. I could be wrong, but I think the mother made a goodbye flight over my house, yesterday. I'm going to miss them, especially the chicks."

"Did all of them survive?" Michael asked, speaking as she knew, from experience, having been an osprey watcher himself. His tales of encounters with these impressive birds had inspired Grace to volunteer.

"Yes, I believe so," Grace replied.

"I guess you know that sometimes the osprey mothers favor one chick over another, and that consequently, some chicks get more food than another. The littlest ones sometimes become weak and the stronger ones bully them. Sometimes even kill them. Sad, but it happens."

"Nature is certainly cruel at times," Bella said.

"But nature can be romantic too," Michael said, clasping his hands together. "Did you know that osprey mate for life? But, if a mate dies, the one remaining will choose another partner for life. See, Grace, there *are* second chances."

Grace smiled. Bella started up her drill, having apparently decided that since there hadn't been any customers for the past half hour, it was a good time to make some noise. Michael neatly folded up the cartons he'd finished with and readied them for recycling.

"Those skaters lanterns are so sweet," Grace said. "Can't you just picture night skating on a pond rimmed with colorful lights like these?"

"I can more than imagine," he assured her. "I skated with one when I was growing up. It had a green glass globe and a chain for carrying and hanging up in the barn when we came home. I wish I had it now, because that particular emerald color is not only incredibly fine but valuable as well. My grandparents owned a number of them and we children had fun skating around with them.

"Sort of like the first flashlights, portable, light weight, and wind resistant," Grace said. "Such nice colors, I like the cobalt one. I purchased a couple of baby skaters, with gadrooned borders. They're still at my house. I'll bring them in soon."

A young couple who were honeymooning on Cape Cod and were puttering around the village, drifted in. Michael asked them about their trip so far, what sights they had seen, where they had been, what their future plans were.

"We bought a condo before the wedding," the young man said. "We don't have a lot of furniture yet."

"Be sure not to forget about lighting," Michael said. "It's not just about practical matters such as reading or cooking. It's about taste, and design and will, undoubtedly, set the mood of your home. You can't go wrong with fine lighting, and antiques can be very affordable. But, whatever you do, don't rely on overhead lighting. Unless you have crystal chandeliers or that type of thing. Overhead lights can be unflattering to your décor, as well as your guests. By the way, where are you young folks from?"

"California."

"Oh. Well, you are probably going to need more guidance than I thought," Michael said, rubbing his chin and frowning slightly.

Grace decided to intervene. What was it about Michael's distaste for California? After all, what did he know of anywhere outside of Cape Cod?

"These cranberry glass lights are pretty," Grace said, holding a small oil lamp with opalescent dots.

"It's gorgeous," the woman agreed. "Remember, Dave, when we toured those cranberry bogs a few days ago?"

"That was fun. We didn't know that cranberries grew in bogs. We thought they grew like blackberries. You know, on bushes."

"You took a tour of cranberry bogs?" Grace asked.

"Yes, I think it was up in Brewster, maybe Harwich," he told her. "It's so confusing around here, the way the towns are kind of melded together."

"I know what you mean," Grace said. "The Cape is like a mystery. You have to use a map and look for clues. Just keep in mind that you can't get too lost, you're never far from water."

"Yeah, we learned that pretty quickly," he said. "We're having a wonderful visit, and we've taken a ton of pictures."

Grace had an 'aha' moment. Tourists took pictures. Maybe the vacationers took pictures the day she was almost run off the road by someone exiting Salty Cove in a big hurry, the day that Ben was murdered.

"Do you by any chance remember the name of the company that you took the tour with?" Grace asked. "I might like to do that myself one day."

As it happened, the young man had the company's card, and cradling it in her hand, Grace determined to follow this lead.

After all, it now appeared that her life might depend on it.

*****

After Grace made a couple of calls from her office, and was getting out her car keys, Audrey appeared, looking a bit ill at ease. She asked Grace what she knew about Beau. "He seems very nice. Handsome too," she added.

"That he is. He's quiet and reserved, but not one of those homicidal loner types," Grace told her.

"Good to know," Audrey said, and let out a laugh. "He asked me if I would help get his bookstore ready for opening."

Beau's a great guy, and he needs *lots* of help up there," Grace smiled, surprised but happy at this latest development. "By the way, I saw Julia last night at a meeting at Portia and Trevor's home. Julia and Roone came by toward the end of the evening. They made it clear they intend to buy Salty Cove from whoever ends up with title to it. I was kind of surprised by Julia. She wasn't particularly friendly. She seemed angry about something."

"Yes. I saw her yesterday," Audrey replied. "She told me that she suspects Roone might be serious about someone else. More than just a casual flirtation. I think she's very stressed out. Anyway, I'll call you later and tell you how the organizing went."

*****

Grace pulled down the shade on the front door. "I'm planning on taking a trip to the cranberry bogs tomorrow," she told Michael and Bella. "Want to come? I could pick you up after church."

"Sure. I'd like to pick up some flyers from the place. It sounds interesting," Bella said. "And, maybe, we can pick up some clues by the roadside where we were almost blindsided."

Grace wasn't surprised by Bella's response. She was keenly aware that thoughts of the day Ben died were still very fresh in her mind.

"We should be done with church and choir by ten thirty," Bella told her.

"Count me in, too," Michael said. "I'd love a quiet Sunday drive."

Grace imagined Michael and Bella as she had seen them on several occasions, in the church loft, Michael's head barely visible to the congregation sitting below, Bella's loud, out of tune baritone, canceling out the softer, modulated voices of the others.

They had been through so much the past week that she was glad she had asked them to join her. Michael was right. A peaceful trip would be a nice respite from all of the trouble they had recently endured.

Chapter Thirty-Nine

Grace lay in her bathtub, bubbles enveloping her in the scent of lavender, a candle bathing the room in a soft glow. Above her, through an open window, she could hear leaves rustling in the night breeze and see a slip of moon peeking in and out through transparent clouds. Clambake napped on a towel that was thrown over a chair, snoring in his cozy big cat way. She'd prefer showering under the stars, but she had promised Andre that there would be no more outdoor showers until the troubling events were over.

As he often did, Frank was reclining in the doorway, one eye closed and the other half open. Apparently hearing a noise, he lifted his massive head about an inch off the ground, long enough for Grace to be certain that asleep or awake, he was listening intently to every night sound.

Feeling that she should get out of the tub, but enjoying the warm water and the relaxation she sank back down into the bubbles for one last minute or two of bliss. She turned on the faucet for another blast of hot water and was gazing fondly at Clambake when she heard a noise at her back door. Frank was already running down the stairs. She froze, her heart pounding until she heard Andre's voice. Only then did she realize that until this murder was solved, she would be living on her nerves.

Chapter Forty

"How'd you know it was me?" Andre said, pouring a cup of decaf coffee and handing it to Grace. He opened her cupboard and chose a mug for himself. He slid the sugar bowl across the counter in her direction.

Grace couldn't help but notice the ease with which Andre was making himself at home in her kitchen. They still hadn't discussed the note he left just a week or so ago. She was grateful for his presence and concern, but she was also purposely keeping him at a safe emotional distance. She felt confused as to what the note meant. Did he really miss her? Was it all about sex? His relationship with Emma appeared to be as chummy as ever. After all, they spent time together in Boston at a conference. She heard stories about police officer conferences. Jack had told her all about some of the things that went on, but she never, for a second, questioned Jack's faithfulness, the way she had Andre's.

"Frank didn't appear to be concerned," Grace said. "He didn't growl and his bark was friendly. How did you get in?"

"You gave me a key months ago, and I must have forgotten to return it," he said, taking a sip of his cop coffee, dark eyes flickering over the rim of his cup.

"How convenient for you," Grace said. "Anyway, I had a cast iron skillet in my hand."

"In the bathroom?"

"You can't be too careful."

Andre laughed.

"So how did it go with Freesia?"

"She's not talking. We did leave her with something to think about."

"What's that?"

"She's a prime suspect in Ben's death and possibly some of the burglaries and assaults that have been going on around here."

"She told me that Ben had a valuable lamp with insects on it and that he gave it to someone. But, I couldn't get any more out of her," Grace said. "I have no doubt she was referring to dragonflies."

"That's more than she told us," Andre said, "Once again, probationers talk more to probation officers than to the cops."

Grace nodded in agreement. "I assume you checked her car. The windshield wiper is broken off. That probably doesn't happen too often."

"We're on top of that," Andre assured her.

"And Mason? Anything new there?"

"We'd like to talk to him again, but he seems to have disappeared," Andre smiled. "Like Petey."

"Poor Petey, out there in the wilds of Cape Cod where he has no business being," Grace said. "I do feel bad for Duane."

"What about Emma losing her beloved pet?"

She didn't have an answer for that, at least not one that she wished to share with Andre.

"I have to go to Provincetown tonight," Andre announced. "My mother needed some minor surgery and I promised I would stay overnight. My dad is laid up with a bad knee, so I don't want to leave them alone. I'd feel better if Bella and Michael stayed with you and Frank for the night.

"With me?" Grace was surprised by the suggestion, but he was right. They shouldn't be alone. "Maybe it would be easier if I went to Michael's house? He isn't too keen on changes."

"Too late," Andre said. "It's all arranged. In fact, here they are now."

Grace looked out her window. Sure enough, Bella's car was in her driveway and the two octogenarians were tumbling out, Bella with two small suitcases and Michael clutching his cat carrier.

"Michael brought Edith? What about Clambake and Frank? Where will I put everyone?"

"You'll figure it out," Andre said. "I've got to go. Emma will keep an eye on you. She's very good at surveillance."

"I bet she is." Grace couldn't stop herself from saying, wondering why Emma was the only officer apparently available for this job.

Andre smiled. "You won't know she's here. I'll be back as soon as I can."

Grace picked up Clambake from his spot on the sofa and carried him upstairs. "Sorry," she told him. "I know things have been strange around here, and now, you will have to stay in my room. Don't worry, it will be all over soon."

And, patting his head, she descended the stairs to greet her latest houseguests.

*****

Frank had been told to stay in the kitchen, and so far, was obeying the command. Michael released Edith to explore the living room. Things were settling down much better than Grace expected, so she offered Bella and Michael, who were relaxing on the loveseat, some ice tea.

"How about a cocktail?" Bella said. "Michael and I have been in the habit of having a sip or two since we've been bunking together."

"A lovely idea," Michael said. "Bella, let's see what Grace has on hand."

Grace followed them into her kitchen where they quickly took charge. Bella marched straight for her pantry and Michael busied himself with the glassware.

"I've got some vodka in the freezer," Grace said, determined to be helpful. "And some cranberry juice. We can make Cape Codders."

Bella emerged with her arms full. Look what I found," she called out.

Grace took the tall shapely bottle from Bella. "It's a liqueur made from elderberries," she said.

"Good," Bella exclaimed, "Now, let me take another look in your refrigerator. Ah, simple syrup. That sounds nice. Do you have lemons?"

"No, but I have a couple of limes."

"Right. Let's do some experimenting. Michael, have you found any decent glasses."

"I think these will be fine," he replied, picking out three martini glasses."

"Oh. It's lemon vodka," Bella said. "Let me see what I can do."

Realizing that Bella and Michael had fallen into what appeared to be a comfortable routine, Grace sat down and let them proceed. She didn't have experience making cocktails. Jack and then Andre having made them on the few occasions that called for libations.

"Now this is a proper cocktail." Michael said. "I really love this."

"Me too," Grace said. "You have to write this down for me. I could drink these all night."

Michael beamed. "What do you say? One more? After all we're not driving anywhere, and it is Saturday night. If we have to be cooped up, might as well make the best of it. We're safe here with Frank."

"And Andre's partner, Emma, is keeping an eye on us, too," Bella said.

If Grace needed one more good reason for another cocktail, Bella had given it to her.

Bella performed her magic again, this time sending Grace out to her garden for some fresh rosemary. "To add a nice herby aroma," she explained.

"I think this needs a name. Got any ideas?' Bella said.

By this time, all rather tipsy, they had a lot of ideas. It took them a half hour to sort through their list and pick a favorite. The Caper.

*****

Grace was beginning to fall asleep when she heard a screeching cat kind of noise. Afraid that something had happened to Clambake, she put on a robe, ran downstairs in the direction of the caterwauling, and found that Clambake and Edith were having a stare down in the dining area. Frank, equally disturbed, had pushed open the door from the kitchen and was barking furiously. Bella was calling to Grace from the top of the stairs. Michael, prone on the sofa, was snoring peacefully but with gusto.

Clambake, most likely sensing that he would like a conversation with Edith, had apparently pried open the bedroom door and padded downstairs, looking for trouble. Now, when Grace tried to grab Edith, hissing and spitting, the old cat managed to scoot behind the sofa. Picking up Clambake, she handed him to Bella, who had joined the fray decked out in a pair of men's red and green plaid pajamas, a couple of hair rollers askew on her head. Returning to find that Frank had cornered Edith and was emitting a low growl, one more cat clearly having pushed him over the edge, Grace took hold of his collar and dragged him to the kitchen.

She patted him on the head, said "Good dog," and jumped when she saw someone peering at her through the back door.

"What's going on?" Emma demanded, pounding furiously. "Open the door."

Grace did as she was told and Frank jumped on Emma, giving her a doggy smooch. So much, she thought, for Frank's loyalties. "Sorry," she said. "Everything is fine. It's just an animal skirmish."

Emma looked around the kitchen where the detritus of their cocktail hour, glasses, limes, and vodka were in plain sight. "Having a party are we?" she said, looking Grace up and down.

"No. No, we were all asleep, when my cat got out of my room," Grace said bristling. Having Emma watch the house was one thing, but having her in the kitchen was another.

"Okay. Glad everyone is safe."

When Frank began barking again, Emma peered through the kitchen window. "Something's on fire!"

"That's my outdoor shower!" Grace exclaimed.

"Got a fire extinguisher?"

"Yes, in the pantry. Here," she said handing it to Emma.

"Get your hose!" Emma yelled as she raced out of the house.

"Call 911!" Grace called to Bella before running to join Emma by the shower. Flames were rising up the sides of the wood enclosure, and sparks were flying toward her roof. Emma aimed foam at the sides nearest the house and had most of the fire under control by the time a fire truck pulled up outside and Firefighters were coming around the side of the house.

After the commotion settled, Grace said, "I'm very grateful that you're here, Emma. Sorry for all the trouble."

"What do you think could have started a blaze over there?" Emma said, tucking a strand of hair behind her ear. "The fire investigators will be back in the morning to take another look. One of them found some matches. Maybe someone's trying to send a very strong message to you and your friends inside."

"More than a message," Grace said, suddenly aware that she was emotionally exhausted. "Looks like someone might be trying to kill us."

Chapter Forty-One

After taking a vote, the threesome decided that the Sunday afternoon drive was still on. The plan was to drop Edith off at her own home, where Michael thought she would be far more relaxed after her difficult night, and Emma had agreed to take Frank with her for the day. Bella insisted on driving, since she needed to get gas anyway. Grace got in the back seat of Bella's antique Volvo, and Michael sat shotgun. The day was hot, and the fact that Bella's air-conditioning emitted only the faintest of cool air didn't help matters. Furthermore, they all were nursing hangovers from the previous night's little party and one too many 'Capers.' Michael and Bella had attended church that morning while Grace stayed home, cleaning up her kitchen and conducting her own investigation around her outdoor shower. She was awake the entire night, pacing her kitchen, drinking coffee until the first light of day, too frightened to sleep. Whoever set fire to her shower must have managed to slip into her yard during the time that Emma was in her kitchen.

When she had taken pictures of her shower for insurance purposes, Grace remembered Sharon, one of the Merry Widows, taking pictures at Salty Cove with her cell phone. Andre hadn't said whether or not they had revealed anything significant. She would ask him. Maybe there was something in those pictures that would shed light on the murder of Ben Walwyn.

Michael wiped his glasses with a tissue, and Grace fanned herself with an old newspaper she found on the backseat. Bella had somehow managed to arrange her unruly hair into a bun of sorts, but a few tendrils, that escaped the knot, were clinging to her neck, glistening and damp. Perched on top of her bun was a pink and black visor decorated with clusters of pearls.

"I like days like this," Michael proclaimed. "Warm and cozy." Grace thought he sounded unreasonably chipper, considering the previous night's activities. But then, Michael had slept through the catfight, Frank's barking, Emma's arrival, and the fire sirens.

"More like hot and steamy," Grace grumbled, staring out the window at a cluster of cottages shimmering in the hazy humid air, one of the many colonies dotting the Cape, that had been built before the onslaught of the fifties era motel boom.

When Bella slowed at an intersection Grace saw a man wearing blue jeans and a black sweatshirt with the hood up, get into a battered white truck and shoot into the traffic ahead of them.

Bella, can you follow that truck?" she said, peering over Bella's shoulder. "I don't know why, but I think that might be the guy that attacked me over in Hyannis Port and stole Mr. Stonely's lamp."

"There are a lot of trucks like that one," Michael said.

"Probably," Grace agreed. "But they all don't give me a shiver up my spine."

The intersection cleared, and Bella tailgated an older model sedan, full of white haired occupants, that was between her Volvo and the truck. After a half-mile or so, the truck began to pick up speed, leaving Bella stuck behind the sedan. Bella let out an exasperated sigh, stepped hard on the accelerator and pulled sharply on her wheel, sending the Volvo into oncoming traffic. Grabbing his arm rest, Michael shouted. "Bellllllaaa!"

"Hush, Michael. This might be the guy who assaulted Grace, and he could be the person who assaulted us!"

"Take it easy, Bella. We don't want to have an accident," Grace cautioned, gripping her seatbelt and holding her breath as the Volvo careened around the slower vehicle, causing Grace to sprawl across the back seat.

"Grace is right," Michael agreed. "We must be careful. And what will we do if we catch up to him?"

"That's up to Grace," Bella replied.

Grace, sitting upright once again, was also wondering what they were going to do. Her best hope was that they could get a glimpse of his license plate, or, even better, that he would pull in somewhere and she could get a closer look at him. "He's slowing a bit. Let's follow for a while and see where he goes," she said.

Turning on to Route 132, the truck picked up speed again. In a matter of minutes the driver sped through a red light and entered a parking lot.

Bella fumed as she stopped at the light. "Did either of you get a glimpse of his license plate? I could have if we hadn't been stuck behind those darn old folks."

"I couldn't see anything," Michael told her. "My eyes were closed most of the time."

I didn't either," Grace said, trying to keep disappointment out of her voice. After all, Bella had tried so hard to catch up to the vehicle. Later she'd tell Andre about the white truck. Not that there was much to tell, since she hadn't caught a good view of the driver, or seen the plate.

"He's going in there," Bella said, pointing at a liquor store. "Let's make a plan. Grace, you and I can follow him. Michael, when I get out, slide yourself over here to the driver's seat and get ready in case we need to skedaddle in a hurry."

When the light turned green, Bella floored it. Roaring into the lot, she slammed on the brakes.

"Bella, are you crazy?" Michael asked, wide-eyed. "That man might be very dangerous. He might have a gun."

"I agree," Grace said, having no desire to put Bella and Michael in harm's way. "Let's wait here and see if we can get a glimpse of him when he comes out."

"He might slip out the back," Bella said, struggling out her door. "Then what?"

Grace jumped out of the back seat and caught up with the swiftly moving Bella. "Here's what we'll do," Bella said, opening the heavy glass door. "I'll go one way, and you go the other. Maybe one of us can recognize him."

Bella moved toward the closest aisle, and Grace raced down the next, hoping to circle around and meet her at the far end. As she turned the corner, she saw Bella, visor pulled low over her face, sidle up to the truck driver and say, "Excuse me. I need to get some champagne from that case."

The man stepped aside without a glance and reached above Bella for a six-pack of beer. His back to Grace, he headed up the aisle toward the check-out counter.

"Let's get out of here, before he sees us," Grace said, pushing Bella through the front door.

"Hey, what do you think you're doing?" the cashier yelled. "You have to pay for that champagne!"

The women froze. Grace felt her already fast beating heart, pound in her chest. The truck driver, digging in his pocket for cash, turned and stared at them.

"Oh goodness. I didn't mean to...," Bella started to say.

"Hurry, get in the car," Grace instructed Bella, who was so rattled by the man's outburst, she dropped the champagne, the pale gold liquid splashing all over Grace's new wedge sandals and drenching Bella's sneakers.

As the cashier came running, Grace reached in her purse, pulled out some bills and threw them at him. "Sorry," she said and taking Bella's elbow thrust her toward the car. Michael was in the driver's seat, staring at them with open mouth.

"Step on it Michael," Bella said, as she climbed in the front seat of her car, and Grace hopped in the back. When Michael proceeded to slowly back up, looking this way and that, Bella said, "Michael, so help me, if you don't get us out of here, I will kill you myself!"

With that, Michael sent them careening into the street. A few horns blared, but Bella told him to ignore them and head for Route 6.

"Is the truck coming this way?" Bella asked.

"He's coming out of the parking lot now," Grace told her, staring out the back window. "Keep going, Michael. We can't let him catch up to us."

"Oh God!" was all Michael could manage.

Grace watched as the truck turned back the way it had come. With a relief that was palpable, she said, "It's okay. Slow down. He's not following us."

Michael pulled to the side of the road. "I'm shaking too much to drive," he gasped.

Bella swung around to look at Grace. "It's Mason Crawford!" she said. "I'm pretty darn sure now that he's the man who came to my house and left me in my bathtub. He has a distinct smell. Sweaty, grassy, and mighty unpleasant."

Grace nodded as she sent Andre a text telling him that Mason was now driving a white truck. She didn't add that she had followed it because of a shiver up her spine. A shiver that hadn't gone away.

Chapter Forty-Two

It wasn't long before they arrived at the building that housed the tour group outfit. The office was a small space and when the three of them entered, two with damp feet that smelled of champagne, they filled up the room.

Grace introduced herself, Bella, and Michael to the young woman, sporting plum colored reading glasses. She wore a nametag that said her name was Karen.

"About a week ago, I was driving by here when a speeding vehicle nearly ran me off the road," Grace told her. "My car almost ended up in the bog with your tour group. Did you, by any chance, witness it?"

"Yes," Karen said. "We were all distracted by the noise. We saw your car swerve to the edge of the road. We were going to check on you, but you pulled away."

"We were scared, but luckily not hurt," Grace said. "Do you, by any chance, remember the other vehicle that was involved?"

"It was a dark color. Maybe black."

Grace felt her heart beat excitedly. "Were you able to see the driver?"

"Oh, no. It happened too fast for that," Karen said, glancing curiously at Bella, who together with Michael, had wandered to a display of brochures where Bella was now stuffing more than a few into her handbag.

"If you remember anything else about the car or the driver, please let me know," Grace said quickly, hoping to get Bella and Michael out of the shop as soon as possible. "Here's my card with my email address."

"Now that I think about it, I may have some photos from that day," Karen said. "I don't know if they would be any help to you, but I could look at what I have when I get home. If there is anything to add, I'll send them to you."

Perhaps, Grace thought with some excitement, this could be the information she needed to get to the truth about what had happened at Salty Cove on that sunny afternoon before she and the Merry Widows had arrived for their sunset picnic.

*****

"We're very close to Salty Cove," Bella said. "It's across the road beyond the bogs. Maybe we should take another look around the property?"

"I'd rather not." Michael mopped his face with his handkerchief.

"Why?" Bella put her hands on her hips. "Are you in a hurry to go somewhere else?"

"No. I'm hungry, and I can think of better things to do than visit a crime scene where a man was murdered by a violent person, who remains, need I remind everyone, at large. Besides, I've read that killers often return to the scene of the crime."

Bella sighed. "You said you wanted to come today."

"Well, I do enjoy a quiet Sunday ride, but I hadn't imagined we'd be involved in a high speed chase."

"What high speed chase?" she demanded, putting the car in reverse. "Honestly, you have such an active imagination."

Chapter Forty-Three

Later that afternoon, as Bella let Grace off and drove away, a rainstorm arrived with full strength, forcing Grace to make a dash for the back door. She was turning her key in the lock to the accompaniment of a roll of thunder when someone grabbed her by her shoulders and she found herself looking into the rough, unshaven face of Mason Crawford.

Once inside her kitchen, he wasted no time telling her he wanted Ben's lamp and if he didn't get it, she and her employees would be in serious jeopardy. He was, he said, tired of wasting his time with all of them.

"I don't know where the lamp is," Grace told him, trying not to sound as terrified as she felt. "You killed your best friend over this. The police are on to you. If you turn yourself in now, it will be better for you."

"I didn't kill Ben. Now, where is the lamp, you have three seconds."

"You killed Ben, and you assaulted my employees. We don't know where the lamp is." Grace stammered trying to buy time, for time was all she had to work with at the moment.

"I didn't kill him!" Mason shouted. "He was my best friend! Now, shut up about Ben! I want the lamp!" The look in his eyes terrified her as much as his words.

"It's at my shop," she told him. "It's under the table where the register is."

Mason pulled duct tape and rope out of his jacket. "You'll stay here in the closet until I get back," he said slapping the tape on her mouth. Grace struggled, but Mason easily overpowered her and propelled her roughly to the small closet under the stairs.

But before he could shove her inside, Bella barged into the house, calling Grace's name in her deep baritone and swinging a tire iron above her head. She charged at Mason without hesitation.

"No theatrics, old woman," Mason growled. "Put that down or I'll take it down!"

Suddenly, from the kitchen, Grace heard Michael yell, "Freeze! It's the police!"

When Mason turned, it was enough of a distraction for Grace to grab the spiky cactus that Felix had brought her and swing it hard at Mason, hitting him in the face. He let out a yelp that left no doubt that the cactus had met its target. Bella stepped up and held the iron rod over his head.

"You want to call me 'old woman,' now?" she said. "Get on the floor before I wallop you."

"I dialed 911," Michael called out, running into the room wielding a carving fork.

Grace took the fork from Michael and sat down hard on Mason's back while Bella leaned over Mason her hands tight around the rod.

"Mason Crawford, It's been a long time, but I remember when you were a little boy, playing with my godson Ben," she said. "Why did you have to kill him?"

Mason squirmed and tried to dislodge Grace from his back, but Michael hopped on and said, "Don't try any tricks, Buster!"

"I should have taken care of all of you, when I had the chance," Mason said. Then having likely realized he wasn't going anywhere but jail, was quiet until police arrived. Officer Gelb and Emma, who held a barking Frank on a leash, were the first officers to arrive. They both appeared alarmed and surprised when they witnessed Grace, Michael, and Bella hovering over the prone suspect, before hauling Mason out of the house.

"Thank goodness you came when you did," Grace said, passing glasses of water to Michael and Bella. "But, why were you here? You only dropped me off a short time ago."

"Michael spotted Mason in the white truck, following us down your street," Bella said. "He saved the day."

Michael beamed at the compliment.

"Thanks to both of you," Grace said. "I'm not sure I would have survived for long in that small closet."

"It's so troubling to believe that Mason murdered Ben," Bella said. "Greed. That's what it was. And the Tiffany lamp is still missing. Perhaps Imogene did something with it without telling anyone."

"We might never know where it is," Michael said

A knock at the door and Grace looked out the window and saw Emma standing on her porch with a very wet Frank.

"Andre is on his way back from Provincetown," she said when Grace opened the door. "He said to bring Frank here and he'd pick him up later. You all okay now? Do you want me to stay?" Frank ran into the room, shook his body and splashed water on all of them.

Michael, looking alarmed at his damp suit, said, "It's time for us to leave, Bella. I need to get home and feed Edith. Do you feel up to driving?"

Bella picked up her tire iron and insisted, in her way that brooked no argument, that she was quite capable of driving in the rain. They promised to call Grace as soon as they arrived at Michael's house. Grace accompanied them out to the car, holding an umbrella over their heads, where they each hugged each other with the hardest, strongest, and most loving hugs that three friends could give.

It was more than a friendship, Grace thought, because they had been there when her life depended on it.

Chapter Forty-Four

Grace dried Frank off in the kitchen, rubbing him down with a beach towel, burying her face in his fur, and feeling a tear slip down her cheek. Thunder and lightning were exploding around the dim room. She felt intense relief that this dreadful episode was now over. Whether the valuable Tiffany lamp was ever found probably didn't matter, but hopefully, Mason's arrest would deter anyone else from causing trouble and would put an end to this nightmare.

She knew they were all lucky to be alive. Mason was no one to mess with. It was certainly possible that Freesia and Mason had conspired together to find the valuable lamp. Freesia might be the one who would talk, and if she did know something, it could answer a lot of questions.

She considered how envy and greed had caused Mason to act as he had. To kill your best friend over money was unfathomable. But Ben had stolen Freesia away from Mason, and from his point of view, maybe that was unforgivable. She had seen firsthand how angry Mason was on that day in front of Pearl's, when he and Ben had fought. He must have followed him home from Pearl's, continued the argument, and then in a jealous rage, shot him. She cringed when she thought about her own jealous feelings toward Emma. Had it been envy or insecurity or did she truly have something to fear? She wasn't about to resort to violence, but she had to admit, her lack of self-confidence might have wrecked her relationship with Andre. She could blame him for making her feel less secure, but it was her responsibility to sort through her own feelings. She winced when she thought about her attempts to make Andre jealous of Felix.

Jealousy was a bad business.

When the lights flickered and went off, she surrounded herself with lanterns and candles. She leaned back on her sofa. Clambake crawled in her lap, made muffins and settled down, while Frank pawed the floor, before lying down by her feet.

Grace couldn't stop thinking about the murder, the assaults, and the still missing dragonfly lamp. There were so many questions. She remembered how fiercely Mason had denied murdering Ben. There was no reason to believe him. After all, he was a brutal man and she believed him to be capable of murder. Still, Ben had been shot, yet Mason hadn't brought a gun into her house and hadn't wielded a gun in his attacks on Bella and Michael.

Grace made herself a cup of strong tea, and not knowing what to do with her nervous energy, decided to check her emails.

Right away she saw one from Karen, the bog tour operator, with attachments of several pictures, each one of which she studied carefully. The six adults and two children on the tour appeared to be enjoying themselves. They posed together; arms wrapped around each other's shoulders, smiling for the camera, each one held a bottle of cranberry juice, dazzling carmine in the evening light.

But there was something else. A shiny black car was visible as it came out of the driveway to Salty Cove. The next photo, which she enlarged, showed her car leaning precariously on the edge of the bog.

That's odd she thought. Mason had a truck and sometimes used Freesia's car. Of course, he could have borrowed or even stolen another vehicle. The day she and Audrey had visited Julia, Roone waved to them from a shiny black car. But why would he be rapidly leaving Salty Cove shortly after the murder? Could it be that he could have been involved in the murder, returned home, and then rushed over when he heard the screams of the Merry Widows?

Her pulse raced as she remembered how Mason and Roone had rescued the osprey. It seemed odd to her, that the sophisticated Roone and violent criminal Mason would be involved in anything together, even a buying trip to purchase plants.

It *was* strange, how the neighborhood was interconnected despite the sociological differences, Grace thought as she forwarded the pictures to Andre, who she knew would have a busy night, processing Mason, trying to get him to make a confession. She wondered what he would think of this new information. She smiled when she imagined the look on his face when he heard about Mason's capture.

She was just pressing 'SEND' when she heard a horn beep in her driveway. Pulling her shades back, and squinting into the darkness, she saw that it was Duane. What in the world, she wondered, was he doing here in the dark in this weather? When he waved to her and pointed in the direction of her barn, she imagined that he was feeling bad about misplacing boxes and losing Petey, and was going to try to sort things out. She waved back at him and indicated that he should come in when he was done and watched the glow from his flashlight skimming the wet ground. And then, he vanished into the dark night.

*****

Chapter Forty-Five

When Frank barked ferociously, Grace told him that it was Duane and not to worry. But then, hearing a loud thump, she opened the door an inch and called out to Duane. There was no response, probably because he couldn't hear her over the howling of the wind. But when there was another thud, she determined to go out and see what was going on. "And, you're staying right here," she told Frank. "I don't want to have to dry you off again."

Pulling on her boots, she put on a rain jacket and dashed into the storm. It was pitch dark, and she knew that the back porch light would guide her only so far. She turned her flashlight on as she approached the barn, shingles glossy in the rain. The sopping grass from her neglected lawn grabbed at her ankles, and the wind propelled an empty flowerpot in her direction, barely missing her feet as she navigated around a puddle by the door.

"Duane?" she called, aiming her light around the cluttered space, illuminating boxes, garden equipment, and lamp odds and ends. Then she heard what sounded like a low moan.

"Duane!" she called when she saw him slumped in a corner. Her heart sank. Duane was clumsy and accident-prone. She should have made him come into the house when she first saw him. She squatted beside him and quickly realized that it was not Duane's clumsiness that caused him to fall. He was barely conscious and a hammer was lying beside his head.

Hearing a noise, she turned only to have two arms clasp tightly around her. She caught a glimpse of a ski mask as her hair was pulled back with such force that she was staring at the barn rafters. Tears sprang to her eyes as she felt hard steel against her temple.

"I'm not letting go," someone told her in a muffled voice, jerking her head back even further. "I don't care if all of your hair falls out. Now, tell me where the damn Tiffany lamp is."

"It's here, Grace gasped, "in one of those boxes by the window. I can show you, but let go of my hair. I can't see anything like this."

"One more time, where is it?" the words were ominous.

"In the back," was all she could manage, and she found herself being dragged around the lawn mower, toward a dark corner.

"Get it!"

"I called the police before I came out here," Grace stammered.

"Then you better hurry."

"It's in the white carton under the eaves."

"If it's not the lamp, I'll shoot you."

Her knees buckled as she was pushed to the ground. The intruder, reaching for the box, gave her the chance that she needed. Scrambling to her feet, she pushed open the back door and sprinted into the marsh.

Chapter Forty-Six

Grace immediately sank up to her knees in mud, and knowing that she was being chased, clutched at some beach grass and pulled herself along in the cold water, cutting herself on the sharp blades. The storm was in full fury now, and she was soaked and shivering. She heard her pursuer gaining on her, and taking a deep breath, she slipped below the surface of the wetlands.

Her heart was hammering, and she thought she would die under the water. But a murderer was searching for her, so she held her breath even though her lungs were screaming for air. When she could no longer go without breathing, she slowly surfaced. Momentarily, she felt disconnected from reality. The night air above the water was as dark and wet as the world below.

She took a breath as quietly as she could. And then, she heard a noise. Peering through strands of tall grass, she thought she saw her pursuer standing about ten feet away. With the ferocity of the storm, the almost total darkness and the roar of the wind she couldn't be sure, so she ducked under the water again, her body aching with cold, sure that she would die in a watery grave, just as Ben had in his swimming pool. The memory of his lifeless body was enough to propel her to the surface again as a crackle of lightening briefly illuminated the marsh and she saw that the person's back was to her. She gulped some air to keep from passing out.

She heard a thunderous splash and realized that whoever it was had apparently fallen into the water. There was an angry cry, some muffled swearing and Grace hoped that the flashlight and gun were gone for good.

She listened as a disturbing quiet descended on the marsh. But, in a few seconds she again heard someone approaching her in the terrible darkness.

If the flashlight and gun were in the water, she realized she might have a chance. She might actually have an advantage since, presumably, she knew the marsh far better than her pursuer. Looking over her shoulder, she saw a dim light indicating what she guessed might be Freezer Road. She wanted to push in that direction, but she was far away, and she figured her pursuer might anticipate that she would go toward the shore and cut her off.

Half swimming, Grace stumbled through the marsh, at times running blindly on mounds of soft, wet earth, and then plunging into deep holes of roiled water. Exhausted, all she could hear was the battering sound of the rain. She had no idea where her attacker was.

Moving blindly, arms outstretched as far ahead as possible, she struggled in the oozing, icy muck until she came to the rickety platforms that led to the osprey nest. Hauling herself up, she stumbled toward the pole thinking that maybe there was a way that she could climb into the nest and hide, her mind clutching at any idea, no matter how insane.

When she heard running footsteps behind her, her feet tangled in sticks and grass a few feet from the pole, and she stumbled and fell hard, her knee cracking on wood. She realized the osprey nest had blown to the ground and she was lying in the jumbled remains. Her hand hit something sharp. She winced, as her palm was pierced. A nail. A nail attached to a small board. She heaved herself up. When her attacker came running, she brought the board down hard, aiming as best she could, using the sound of heavy breathing as her guide, at what she hoped was the pursuer's head. There was a thud as a body hit the ground.

Grace heard an angry moan. She dropped the board and was feeling around for it when she felt hands go around her ankle and bring her down. She fell on her back. She once again felt a gun barrel against her temple.

"I killed Ben, and I will kill you, too," a familiar voice told her. "I was able to keep my gun out of the water, so don't even think it doesn't work."

"Julia?" Grace stammered.

"Where's the Tiffany lamp?" Julia demanded. "It's worth a fortune, and I want it. If you cooperate, I'll drive you far away and drop you off in the middle of nowhere. By the time you find your way out of the wilderness, I'll be in another country."

"You killed Ben?"

"It's simple, Grace," Julia said. "I had an affair with Ben. I told you I was attracted to him. He was a wonderful lover, the best ever. But then, out of the blue, he told me that he's back with that low life Freesia Foster. I mean, Freesia or me? Really?"

"I think your bluffing," Grace said. "You didn't kill Ben and you're not going to kill me. Put the gun down, Julia, and let's sort this out."

"I killed Ben because he insisted on dumping me for that little scumbag. He wouldn't listen to me. We argued, and he told me to beat it. He stood at the edge of his pool and smirked at me, as though he didn't have a care in the world. That's when I shot him. He made his choice. And now, I think I deserve the final prize. Roone told me how valuable the lamp is."

"So Roone was involved too?"

"Of course not. He's an unfaithful husband, but basically he's a wimp."

"But you must have had an accomplice."

"I hooked up with Mason Crawford. Granted he's not my type, and I had to sleep with him in order to control him." Julia was silent for a minute. "Ben was special, and I did love him."

"Did Mason know you killed Ben?"

"No. The less he knew the better."

While Julia was talking, Grace groped about for another board, anything that she could surprise Julia with if she had the chance. Her hands found a rock and figuring she had nothing to lose, she struck out in Julia's direction, but Julia deflected the blow and struck Grace with her gun.

The pain was razor-sharp, and Grace felt herself drifting

into unconsciousness. She imagined soft fur brushing her face. Was it an angel wing? She must be dead. She saw a light and felt relief course through her body. Maybe being dead wasn't so bad after all.

Suddenly, she heard ferocious growling followed by a loud scream. What felt like an animal paw scraped her face, as Julia thrashed on the ground beside her.

"Miss Tolliver!"

"Duane!" Bringing her semi-conscious self into the light from Duane's lantern, Grace managed to shout, "She has a gun!"

She heard the brutal sound of fist landing on flesh as Duane grappled with Julia, who was apparently fighting back with everything she had. In the lantern's flickering light, Grace could see that Frank, growling ferociously, had Julia's arm securely in his mouth, and then, there were more lights, and Andre was pulling Duane off of Julia.

"It's okay. She's not going anywhere now," Andre said, as he helped an unsteady Duane to his feet. Julia, finally limp and quiet, was being cuffed by Emma.

Grace was in terrible pain, but she knew in that instant that Duane and Frank saved her life. As she began to drift away again, she felt a warm hand on her cheek. "Gracie," Andre said, "It's over."

Chapter Forty-Seven

Grace sat cocooned on her loveseat, wrapped in her robe, topped with a cushy light coverlet, sipping the scotch that Andre handed her,

"I brought over some *tarte de amenden*," he said. "Want a piece?"

"When did you have time to make an almond tart?"

"About 2:00 a.m.," he told her. "I couldn't sleep. Crushing nuts made me relax."

Although she had taken a hot shower to wash Julia and the marsh mud out of her hair, she felt cold. Her cottage was dim; the power was still out, the wind still howling. An oil lamp burned on the table next to her and Andre had placed a number of candles around the room.

"I'll pass on the dessert for now," Grace said. "I have so many questions. For starters, who do you think killed Ben?"

"Julia confessed to you, but a check of her gun will reveal a lot. Ben more than likely realized that he was in deeper than he wanted to be with someone who would never love him."

"Julia told me she loved *him*."

"I think she was getting a thrill out of having a secret affair with a neighbor right under her cheating husband's nose. Maybe it was revenge, maybe jealousy."

"Go on," Grace said.

"After you sent me the pictures from the tour group, I stopped by Roone and Julia's house on my way back from Provincetown," Andre continued. "Roone had quite a lot to say when I showed him the pictures of the black Mercedes leaving Salty Cove. He acknowledged that it was his car, but denied that he was in it at the time. He said that he'd recently become suspicious that his wife might be having an affair with Ben. After following her over to Salty Cove one day, he apparently got an eyeful. He admitted lying when he said she was home making dinner after the murder, because he was certain that she had nothing to do with Ben's death and he didn't want to get involved. He was afraid their personal lives would become public once her affair became known. But after I pressed him, he acknowledged that she was driving his car that day. It seems that she had offered to take it to the carwash."

"Too bad he didn't come forward with this a week ago," Grace said.

Andre nodded. "He also said that Julia had been a suspect in the death of her first husband, who apparently died after falling off a cliff in Nepal. She was never charged, and he saw no reason to doubt her. He said he hadn't given it much thought."

"Julia told me that it was Roone's wife that died in Nepal."

"We'll be investigating the Nepal incident in time. She may have been trying to link Roone and murder in your subconscious. He also said Julia went out last evening around the same time your shower was set on fire.

"What about Freesia? Was she involved in any of this?"

"Freesia says she attempted to break into the lamp shop, because Mason told her that, if she didn't, he would tell the police that she killed Ben. We'll be talking to her again tonight. We don't know how involved she is, or, if in fact she had anything to do with the murder. There's a lot to sort out, and maybe Freesia will be the one to fill in the gaps. As for Mason, Bella is quite sure that he's the one who attacked her at her place. Unfortunately, Michael can't tell us anything about his attacker. We're thinking it was probably Mason who burglarized Salty Cove."

Andre carefully traced the bandages that covered her face with his finger. "Better get some rest," he said. "I've got to go over to the station, but we need to talk. I have some things I want to say to you. Maybe there'll be a chance tomorrow, depending on how things go with the investigation tonight.

Meanwhile, I've called Audrey and she is on her way over here to keep you company. Frank will be here too."

Grace leaned over and wrapped her arms around Andre. His first response was clearly one of surprise but then, she felt his lips on hers. It was a long kiss, the kind Grace knew she would never forget.

There was a rap on the back door. Andre pulled slowly away from her, and with obvious reluctance went to answer it.

Seconds later, Duane loped into her living room. "Duane, you're a hero!"

Duane beamed. "Glad I was there to help."

"What about your head?" Grace asked. "You've got some nasty looking cuts and bruises."

After assuring her that he had been "stitched up," as he put it, Duane related what happened after he'd looked for the missing boxes in the barn, as well as how Julia got the drop on him. When he came to, he'd heard Frank barking and managed to get over to the house and let him out. After calling 911, he'd followed Frank into the dark marsh. Once there, he didn't know who he was fighting. He only knew he had to win. "She's one strong lady," he said.

Just then, the back door slammed, and Felix came sauntering in, soaking wet, frizzy hair plastered to his head, wearing baggy shorts, his sandals dripping on the floor.

"What a storm!" he exclaimed. "Power been out for long? What's been going on here?"

"It's a long story, Felix," Grace told him. "I'll tell you about it tomorrow."

Andre leaned down, his eyes twinkling in the candlelight like fireflies at dusk.

"So, *that's* your hunky houseguest?" he whispered. "You've got some explaining to do."

Grace was still too disoriented by his kiss to ask him what he was talking about, although, of course, she knew.

Chapter Forty-Eight

Grace stumbled out of bed at dawn, having barely slept. It would take time for the fear engendered by last night's events to subside. Not that she was afraid anymore, but the memory of being pursued by Julia in the marsh would take time to heal. Her recollection of Duane's bravery made her smile. There were some who advised her not to hire him last year, and now he had saved her life. She owed him far more than she could ever hope to repay.

Opening her window, she breathed in the salty Cape air. The storm had left the marsh battered, but today, the water twinkled in the silky light. The osprey pole, which she ran to last night, was bare, the nest resting on the ground where she fought violently with Julia. It occurred to her now that the board she used to hit Julia was probably from the nest. Thank goodness for the Ospreys tendency to hoard miscellaneous garbage, which had bought her some valuable seconds.

The door to Felix's room was open but he was nowhere to be seen. Andre had seemed surprised by the sight of Felix and rather amused, probably because Felix in the flesh was not likely to inspire jealousy.

She smelled the comforting aroma of breakfast. On her kitchen table were scrambled eggs, muffins, and blueberry jam. Frank and Clambake had been fed and coffee was brewing.

"Good morning!" Audrey said. "Felix left a little while ago. He said he has a surprise for you."

"Uh oh. What kind of surprise?"

"I don't know. He said he'd catch up with you later today."

"I *do* need to thank him for that ugly cactus," Grace told

her. "I was going to plant it behind the shed, but now, it deserves a place of honor, perhaps near the shower when I get it rebuilt. I bet Mason is still picking out thorns and spikes."

"I certainly hope so," Audrey said. "Listen, Grace why don't we hang out here today, relax, read books, and talk. You look pretty beat up."

Grace looked in the little mirror hanging by the back door, and grimaced. "That sounds wonderful. But I can't. I have to go to the shop and work on that large project for the inn."

"No, you're not. I took the liberty of calling Michael, Bella, and Duane and told them that Pearl's would be closed today. Bella mentioned she was feeling a mite tired herself, and was going to stay at her own house and unwind without Michael telling her what to do every other minute. So you see, you're stuck with me and I've decided we're going to stay here."

"But..."

Audrey held up her hand to silence Grace. "Bella also told me that she and Michael will be at Pearl's at six tonight and you can join them to work on the order. It sounded like a command to me."

A command, which Grace was quite happy to follow.

Chapter Forty-Nine

Precisely at six, Grace and Audrey arrived at Pearl's, glowing in the early evening, a mix of setting sun and colorful glass lamps. They carried bags of sandwiches and salads from the Barnstable General Store, and Audrey went directly to the kitchen to get some plates.

Bella was up to her elbows in rolls of white linen which she was cutting for shades. Beside her, to Grace's surprise, her father, wearing a starched apron, was busy polishing a silver plated lamp and humming a zippy old tune along with Bella.

Michael was at one of the large pine tables, with an assortment of shades lined up for trimming, instructing Gink, in his most officious voice, how to choose the right trim and how to cut it to fit the shade. Gink, for her part, looked somewhat annoyed, but to Grace's great relief, sober. It was clear to Grace that she would definitely need support to continue with her sobriety. Fortunately, Duane said he would keep close tabs on her.

Sophie, who, with Stanley on her lap, was sitting at another table surrounded by a large number of colorful finials, told Grace that Bella had asked her to pick out styles with a Cape Cod theme to top off the lamps. Duane was getting boxes ready to pack up the lamps and shades when they were completed. As usual, Clay was doing nothing other than walking around scattering crumbs from Michael's brownies all over the recently vacuumed floor.

When Beau arrived soon after, he hurried to the kitchen to give Audrey a hand, blushing when Michael let out a friendly chuckle.

Naturally, the conversation was about the upheaval of the past few days. There was a sense of relief that the perpetrators of such awful crimes were behind bars, and everyone complimented everyone else on their bravery and courage. But, Grace knew Bella, Michael and Duane were the only real heroes. Tears sprang to her eyes when she remembered Bella and Michael springing into action and getting the best of Mason. As for Duane, he had surely saved Grace's life. After Julia hit her in the temple with the gun, she had known that she had nothing left to fight with.

Bella mentioned that when William stopped by a short time ago, he had been horrified by hearing the details of the arrests and learning that Julia Seymoor, Ben and Imogene's neighbor, had most likely killed his brother. He said he wasn't all that surprised by Mason Crawford's involvement, and often thought that he was a bad influence on Ben. He and Morgan decided they were not going to be a part of any lawsuit against Owen for a share of the estate, particularly since it would hardly be a way to welcome Owen to the family. He wasn't sure what Portia and Trevor were planning. They were grasping at any possible way to avoid a jail sentence for Trevor and had mortgaged their home to make a show of good faith. They weren't ready to meet with Owen, let alone consider him their nephew, but he was holding out hope that in time, they would all be one happy family again, an idea that made Bella roll her eyes in disbelief.

William had further suggested to Bella that she talk to Owen about the provenance of the Tiffany lamp, saying that he hoped that if it was located, it would be returned to the original owners, or at least their heirs. As for the future of Salty Cove, that would be up to Owen.

Audrey and Beau brought out the snacks and drinks and set them down on Bella's counter. Grace grinned when she saw her father grab a sandwich just seconds before Duane.

"There's enough for everyone," Audrey said. "There's more in the refrigerator."

"Do you have egg salad?" Michael inquired. "That's my personal favorite."

"Sure do," said Beau, putting one on a plate and bringing it to Michael. "Want something to drink?"

"I'll get it myself in just a spell," Michael told him. "Gink needs my full attention right now."

Apparently Gink overheard him if her looks- could -kill expression was any indication. Duane handed her a sandwich in the nick of time.

"By the way, Beau," Michael said, not realizing that he had just had a near death experience. "Didn't you mention recently that you came across some lamp books when you were organizing upstairs? Why don't you bring them down and maybe they will help me explain things to Gink."

"Sure. I'll be happy too," Beau said. "Audrey, want to help me?"

Grace, along with everyone in the room, except Sophie, who was too young, and Clay who was too self-absorbed, watched as Audrey and Beau left through the front door, on their way to climb the stairs to Beau's Books. They made a cute couple, Grace thought and she didn't expect to see them back downstairs for quite some time. Love, anticipation and hope were in the air, and Grace remembering Andre's kiss, felt her stomach turn over with excitement. Setting her feelings aside, she continued painting a shade with frolicking whales, a bright sky and soft clouds until it looked suitably Cape Coddy to her.

The plan was to stay as late as possible, so they could collectively make a dent in the order of thirty custom shades that Grace promised Tia. They wouldn't finish, of course, but they had all agreed to get together as often as needed to get the job done.

Time blew by like a swift sea breeze, and Grace was surprised when she saw the old clock on the wall, indicate that it was after eleven. She was feeling sleepy but content, until Felix, accompanied by a young woman similarly dressed in shorts and a tee shirt, arrived. Introducing his companion as Christy, he explained that they had met at the writer's conference, and he had exciting news to share.

Grace was momentarily taken aback. Yes, love might be in the air, but had Felix, her eccentric houseguest, been shot by cupid's arrow, too?

"I wrote an article about Pearl's and the unusual people who work here," Felix said holding Christy's hand. "I submitted it to a Cape magazine and they're going to publish it! It will have photos of the shop and the lamps and everyone. Isn't that cool?"

Grace was stunned. It hadn't occurred to her that Felix could actually write. Getting published, she knew was so difficult. How had he managed? He hadn't impressed her as someone who would accomplish anything that remotely challenging. So, there was love, anticipation, and excitement for Felix, too, and she was happy for him.

Clay wanted to know if he would be featured as well, since he was an important client of Pearl's and was acquainted with many prominent customers in the community. Before Felix could answer, Bella interrupted with offers of sandwiches to Felix and Christy. Clay, apparently picking up on Bella's obvious distraction, slunk off to the plate of rapidly disappearing brownies, where Sophie was busy wrapping a few in napkins and putting them in her pockets. Clay glared at her, and then proceeded to do the same thing.

Grace's stomach flipped when Andre suddenly appeared. Not having expected him, she was thrown off balance by his arrival. Clumsily, she dripped a dollop of blue paint into her carmine creating a striking purpley color.

Andre moved through the room, greeting everyone, with a particularly long hug for Bella, Then he slowly, too slowly, Grace thought, made his way over to her painting table. Leaning down, he whispered, "When you're finished here, we're going somewhere."

"We are? It's very late."

"Doesn't matter. It's never too late to go to the beach."

Grace smiled. She was sure she'd heard Andre say the same thing, one evening last winter when he had invited her to his house. Dinner was followed up by a dark, cold and memorable trip to Sandy Neck.

Audrey and Beau finally returned, looking tousled and flushed in a beguiling way, having been gone, as Grace had expected, for a long time. Beau explained that they had needed to do a lot of searching in order to find those books for Michael.

"Of course you did," Bella said with a chuckle.

"Laugh all you want, folks," Beau said, placing a stack of books on the table, "but, we had to climb into the loft to do a thorough search."

"We found something very, very interesting, tucked away under the eaves," Audrey said handing a box to Bella.

"For me?" Bella pushed her glasses up on her nose.

When Grace's stomach did another more serious flip, she jumped up and quickly went to Bella's work area. It could only be one thing, she thought.

Beau untied the string wound tightly around the package and Bella peered inside. "Oh, my goodness!" Her hand flew to her chest, and she sat down on her stool. She looked around at everyone.

"Hurry, take it out of the box," Michael demanded.

"Yes, please, Bella," Clay said, elbowing his way closer to the counter.

Bella, with Beau's help, carefully lifted the beautiful bronze lamp with the shade of dragonflies, their heads, with blue-green eyes, dangling over the curved edge, and set it on her counter, where everyone could see it.

"Ooooh," Sophie said, dropping Stanley to the floor. "That is so pretty."

"But how did it..?" Bella asked, glancing at Duane.

"Whoa, sorry, my system must have broken down." Duane hung his head. "Darn! Why can't I do anything right?"

Grace put her arm around his shoulders. "Duane, you don't need to apologize," she assured him. "The lamp is not the reason Ben was killed. And, if you hadn't misplaced it, it would be gone forever. It would never be returned to its rightful owners."

"That's right, Duane, I'd say your system worked," Bella said.

"Me, too," Michael piped up

"Folks, I'd like to have a small tribute to my godson, Ben," Bella said. "Does anyone have a match?"

Michael opened a drawer where candles for the oil lamps were stored. "What do you want these for?" he asked, handing her a box of them.

Bella held up a cigar. "Michael, please. A light if you don't mind. Now, would anyone else like to join me?"

Duane spoke first, "Sure, Captain Bella. Why not?"

There were murmurs of approval as Michael ambled around with a match, lighting a cigar for everyone.

"To Ben," Bella said, after taking a puff. "Ben was a good man. He had his problems and made his mistakes, but I knew him from the day he was born, and he was a sweet child and devoted to his mother, Imogene. May his soul rest in peace."

"To Ben," everyone echoed her. Grace hated cigars, especially the smell, but she would do anything for Bella, she told herself as she inhaled, only to be overtaken by such a spell of coughing that Audrey ran to the kitchen for some water.

"Thank you all for indulging me," Bella said. "You're all family to me. And that includes you too, Clay."

In response, Clay raised his cigar, faint tears visible in his eyes, which surprised Grace because she hadn't thought him capable of any genuine emotion.

"Michael and I have a surprise too," Bella went on to announce. "I was feeling a tad unsettled the other day and came to realize that I missed the fun I had staying at Michael's house. He's agreed to leave Cape Cod for one weekend and go to Boston with me. I'm taking him to the gardens and museums, and if we have time, we'll hop over to Cambridge."

This time, it was Michael's turn to blush. "I agreed because Bella says we can take the ferry from P-Town and we won't have to go over the bridge," he said.

Andre's cell phone rang. He nodded and handed it to Duane. "It's for you."

Duane, looking anxious, said, "Hello?"

"Uh huh, Yup, Uh huh," he said.

"Everything okay?" Grace asked him.

He broke out in a grin that lit up his entire face. "That was Emma. Petey's been found. He's alive!"

Everyone's mouth dropped open.

"I put a notice on Craig's List. Petey flew all the way to Chatham. Emma says he's in fine shape."

"Found birds, discovered lamps! I think we need champagne!" Clay said, looking around at everyone with a hopeful look on his face.

"I've got some in my car," Andre said.

"Now that's the ticket!" Bella said.

"I second that," said Grace's father. "Listen, son, none of my business, but is it customary for police officers to carry champagne in their official vehicles?"

"Special occasions allow for it," Andre said with a wink.

Chapter Fifty

Leading the way down the stairs to the beach, Andre guided Grace with his flashlight. Near midnight, the moon cast a buttery glow on the bay and stars crowded the sky like sprays of fine sugar.

A dreamy breeze blew southward over Sandy Neck and Cape Cod Bay wrapping itself around the two as they huddled together on a beach blanket. Andre was well prepared for this excursion; his backpack was stuffed with all manner of goodies including lobster rolls, coleslaw, french bread and chocolate chip cookies.

"Hungry?"

"I shouldn't be, I've been nibbling all night, but those lobster rolls look fabulous."

"How about some champagne to wash it all down?" Andre asked. "After all, Clay drank two thirds of the bottle I brought to Pearl's."

"Of course he did," Grace said. "Clay will eat or drink anything to excess, as long as he's not buying."

Andre laughed. "Maybe Felix should include Clay in his article. He certainly is one of a kind," Andre said, popping the cork.

"That he is," Grace agreed.

"Speaking of one of a kind, your dad asked me to tell you he'll be at your house early tomorrow morning," Andre said.

"Did he say why?" Grace asked, as she ceremoniously clinked her glass with Andre's.

"He's bringing his sheep over to take care of your lawn. Munch, munch," Andre said, indicating a grasping mouth with his hand.

"No!"

"Yes." Andre's eyes flickered with amusement. "I really like your dad. He's got so much spirit."

"That he does," Grace said. "I just never imagined he'd become a shepherd."

"That was a nice gesture of remembrance Bella gave for Ben," Andre said.

"Yes, except for the cigars. Ugh!" Grace wrapped her arms around her knees. "I've been thinking about how I might make a tribute to Ben. I only met him once, and didn't particularly care for his manner, but he didn't deserve to die like that. Maybe I'll check in on Freesia now and then, when she gets released, if she'll let me. After all, Ben *did* love her and now he's gone and her backup boyfriend is going to be in jail for quite a while. And we did bond over her version of a gin cocktail."

"Yes, I'd say you did." Andre pulled her closer. "That's a nice thought. Glad you haven't lost your faith in humanity."

"It's been tested, for sure," she said wistfully.

"Let's talk," Andre said. "I'll get right to the point. I want us to try again. I've missed you. I haven't known how to approach you. But now it seems that circumstances have conspired to bring us into the same orbit again."

Grace laughed. "I bet there aren't too many couples that can claim a murder brought them together.

"Twice," Andre said, laughing, too.

They both stared into the night, the stars, and the sea.

"Emma and I are just partners," Andre said. "I know I haven't made you feel secure in the past. I promise to do better. I was trying to balance the two of you. I know now balance is not the right way to go. I hope that someday you might be comfortable enough with each other to be friends. She's a good person."

"I know she is, although I'm not sure that makes me feel better," Grace admitted. "I'm sorry I used Felix to make you jealous. It's such an awful feeling. I wonder, does everyone feel jealous?"

"Sure, I think everyone does at one time or the other. I suppose, there are some that don't, but I'm not sure I would want to be one of them."

"I think there's normal jealousy, and crazy, dangerous jealousy. It can certainly get out of control, like with Julia." Grace took a sip of champagne. "Ben and Mason had years of feuding over Freesia, letting jealousy interfere in their friendship. Like the osprey parents who favor one chick over another, sibling rivalry can begin with jealousy. William and Portia certainly have their issues."

"It's all about possessiveness and control. At least in the human world."

"Yes," Grace said. "Let's promise never to let things get to that point."

Andre pulled her in close, and buried his face in her neck. Cookies, half eaten lobster rolls and coleslaw rolled into the soft sand. They kissed for long time, making up for the past months without each other.

"*Destino,*" Andre whispered, as they collapsed into the folds of the warm beach blanket and watched the moon and stars, satellites and clouds, until they fell asleep in each other's arms.

The End

About the Author

Patricia Driscoll is a retired San Francisco probation officer. She has had a love affair with all things Cape Cod, since her first summer spent on the sands of Craigville Beach. She presently lives in northern California.

Praise for "Shedding Light on Murder," book one in the Grace Tolliver Cape Cod Mystery Series.

"Driscoll's entertaining debut introduces ex-probation officer Grace Tolliver, new owner of Pearl's Antique Lamps and Shades…the suspense builds to a riveting confrontation. Replete with authentic Cape Cod settings, this cozy should have wide appeal." Publishers Weekly

"…an appealing sleuth, an intriguing plot and a picturesque locale." Carol Thomas- Mystery series Examiner.

"…a warm winter read…Grab a cup of cocoa and settle in." Barbara Clark-Barnstable Patriot.

Contact her at www.patriciadriscoll.com
Facebook

The Caper

1 oz. Lemon Vodka

1oz. St. Germaine Liqueur

¾ oz. Cranberry juice

½ oz. simple syrup

Squeeze of fresh lime

Shake in cocktail mixer ice. Strain, garnish with a fresh sprig of rosemary, and serve in an up glass.